Commentary For the New Pastor

Now that you ar there, What's next?

Commentary for the New Pastor
Now that you are there, what's next?

Bishop Marc L. Neal

FOREWORD BY BISHOP ALFRED A. OWENS JR.

© 2003 by Marc L. Neal. All rights reserved.

Printed in the United States of America

Previously this book was written and known as." Did God send you or did the members call you." With a new vision we maintain the same consistantcy with the name change.

No part of this publication may be reproduced, stored in a retrieval system, or transmitted in any way by any means—electronic, mechanical, photocopy, recording, or otherwise—without the prior permission of the copyright holder, except as provided by USA copyright law.

Unless otherwise noted, all Scriptures are taken from the the King James Version of the Bible.

Scripture references marked NASB are taken from the New American Standard Bible, © 1960, 1963, 1968, 1971, 1972, 1973, 1975, 1977 by The Lockman Foundation. Used by permission.

Scripture references marked tlb are taken from The Living Bible, Copyright © 1971 owned by assignment by Illinois Regional Bank N.A. (as trustee). Used by permission of Tyndale House Publish-ers, Inc., Wheaton, Illinois 60189. All rights reserved.

ISBN-13: 978-0692617106 (Marc L. Neal)

ISBN-10: 0692617108

Dedication and much thanks to....

This summation of material regarding the new Pastor and his Ministry is dedicated first to my Lord and Savior Jesus Christ; who has enabled me, and counted me faithful by putting me into the ministry. Thank you Jesus, I would not want to be anywhere else or be in any other profession! Next, I would like to dedicate this book to my family, who unfailingly prayed for me and supported me from the very beginning, while I preached to seven people though now while I preach to crowds of three thousand and more. Lastly, to my maternal grandparents who are now deceased (Deacon William L. & Hattie Neal), thank you for making us go to church.

Special thanks to my co-editors Kristin B. Ward and Kristina M. Stockton thank you for your time and professionalism, you are both truly God sent. May the grace and prosperity of God shower you materialistically, financially, emotionally, but most of all spiritually. To my sister Marletta Jean Lewis, thanks for the initial red ink, take care of my nephews—the first print of the book is finally completed.

Lastly, it is dedicated to every new Pastor in Ministry and those aspiring to be. May you find favor and peace in the eyes of God as you fulfill his purpose in your life and remember, it is good to know that God sent you to pastor a ministry, instead of the members having called you.

Table of Contents

Foreword 9
Preface 13
Pastoral Acknowledgements 17
Introduction 19
The Definition of the Term Church And Its Types 27
Did God Send You, or Did the Members Call You? 35

Chapter 1: The Doctrinal Statement 47
Chapter 2: Church Ordinances 57
Chapter 3: Ministers, Evangelist, Missionaries,
  Associates, and Elders 67
Chapter 4: Church History....................................79
Chapter 5: Prayer Service 85
Chapter 6: Finances 93
Chapter 7: Church Membership 103
Chapter 8: Sick and Shut in 109
Chapter 9: Visitors 115
Chapter 10: Keys 121
Chapter 11: Parking Lots 127

Chapter 12: Church Supplies 133
Chapter 13: Church Store Accounts 139
Chapter 14: Church Mail, Mail Boxes and Email 145
Chapter 15: Offsite Church Property 151
Chapter 16: Deacons And Trustees 159
Chapter 17: Secretaries 167
Chapter 18: Van Ministry 175
Chapter 19: Compensation for Employees 181
Chapter 20: Expectation of the Pastor 187

Questions that are generally asked by the Pulpit
  Committee, Search Committee, Church
  Council or Deacon ministry 197

Read What Other Pastors Are Recommending 201

Foreword

In the Church age where the paradigm of pastoral ministry has shifted from mediocre supervision and direction to brilliant church management and administration, it deliberately has been because of the continual vision of the senior pastors and how they have intimately and intensely saturated themselves in the presence and anointing of the Lord. It is true that pastors cannot advance Kingdom ministry for themselves or the people that God has placed them over with out the power and favor of Jehovah God. Although a pastor is endowed with God's grace and mercy, there are four things that I am convinced that pastors should relate spiritually to their life as they acknowledge their pastoral call.

First, each pastor must be spiritual, which is different than emotional. In order for pastors to spiritually teach, preach and reach the congregation where they serve, they must be spiritually connected with their source of anointing which is Christ. Secondly, all pastors must uncompromisingly and assertively

Commentary for the new Pastor

equip themselves academically. No leader should be satisfied with possessing general working knowledge amidst a society that has generously and liberally provided literature, computer software, commentaries and more for his or her retention. Every pastor must study. Thirdly, each pastor must display godly leadership in order to convince, convert and correct those who will submit to his or her leadership. If a pastor fails to be spiritual, fails to equip him or herself academically and provide sound leadership, he or she should not entertain a congregation for pastoring. Lastly, each pastor needs this book.

Throughout the material listed Pastor Neal has stressed the need for the man or woman of God, who has accepted the responsibility of pastoring to know of a certainty that God has sent him or her to a particular ministry and he or she have not simply answered the voice of the local church members. He has also convincingly argued the need for each pastor to know what he or she is to do once he or she arrives at his or her post for ministry. Surely each pastor must know what he or she is to do once he or she begin to pastor. Undeniably, pastoring is not going to be a table full of peaches and cream or apple pie and ice cream. But if each pastor has aggressively prepared him or herself spiritually, academically and commonly, it will make the pastorate that much more enjoyable, as well as honorable. My prayer for you the reader is to first continue your relationship with the Lord as a Christian, to pursue a strong educational career and most of all be a spiritual combat leader, all the while spiritually liberating the people of God. May you uncover evidence and

Foreword

reasons to reevaluate and verify your call to ministry, while gaining knowledge on what to do once you assume your role as pastor.

Ever so Faithful to Christ,
Bishop Alfred A. Owens Jr.
Pastor, Mt Calvary Holy Church of America Inc.
Washington, DC Author, Sermons for Victorious Living

Preface

Did God send you or did the members call you to the Ministry where you are serving as Pastor? Well, I expect that you are qualified to answer that question. If not now, hopefully by the time you have completed this book, the origins of your calling, and administrative ability will have been made clear. Every pastor and minister, who has gripped the plough for ministry, should be able to recite and recall his/her *"calling"* from God into the Gospel Ministry. (As a matter of fact, not only should each pastor have the ability to do this, but also know with a certainty of his or her area of Ministry that God has commissioned him or her to, especially if it is to the pastorate). Let's concur that God has endowed you with the gift of interpreting and orating His word as a Pastor, and let's say you are now at your first pastorate (*or rekindling the pastorate where you are*). What do you do now that you are there? Yes, I know you should "preach", and you know you should "preach", as a matter of record the congregation is

Commentary for the new Pastor

hoping that you can "preach", but what else, what is next? Is preaching all that the pastor is responsible to do?

Unfortunately, just preaching is all that a lot of pastors throughout the country have resorted to because they are unsure of who commissioned them to serve where they are and what to do once they began their first pastorate. And now, instead of building and developing their Ministry, they are fighting clique fires and gossip. For if they were sure that God sent them, they would invest more of their time in administration than aggravation. Once a new pastor arrives to the Ministry that God has sent him or her to, they are to administrate and set things in order that are spiritually deficient in the church.

Personally, I learned pastoring the hard way *(through experience)*, and because of this, I have discovered several techniques that each pastor/shepherd should know prior to going into a new pastorate/pasture (especially if a hireling has previously been there). Permit me to confess, that there are church related topics that no one discussed with me, which I eventually found out on my own. In this book, there is information, morals, and ideals that I believe God has poured into me, that I might pour into others, that each minister may become better equipped to serve where they are. I believe that each Man and Woman of God is to effectively and successfully minister to and over the Church of God to produce fruit that will remain. Naturally, there were influential people supporting me, but my best teacher has been experience. Therefore, in these chapters you will read about the Church and her biblical definition and issues to consider once you exercise the mantle passed to you at your new place of worship. Once you complete this book, you will come to know why it is so important to understand your call to ministry, church doctrinal

Preface

statements, the various ordinances within the local church, the church history and especially the up-keeping of the visitor and membership information.

Furthermore, this book provides for you notable suggestions to consider for church administration once you have begun your tenure as Senior Pastor, and other relevant tips to acquaint yourself with. Others may have off-handedly mentioned, but not strongly enough alluded to the importance of things such as: the church finances, the mail and mail box, the church property, the authority of the deacons and trustees, compensation of employees, what the real expectations and responsibilities of the pastor are, and what the possible myths will surface as. If you don't know these items, as well as others listed in this book, your first pastorate may be a nightmare or cause you to question if God actually sent you there now that the members don't want you there.

Knowing some of these topics or areas of administration and being able to apply them to your life and ministry can assist you in bringing clarity to determining if God sent you to that particular ministry, or if the members who were so excited *(like you)* issued a call and you then responded to them. One of the worst things that can occur in the life of a Pastor is to react to the voice of the people instead of hearing and then responding to the voice of God. Answer this question, whose voice did you heed? Well, at any rate, now that you are the Senior Minister what's next? Do you know what issues to consider when pastoring? Do you know how far to go and where to begin when addressing spiritual issues regarding your flock?

The best advice I can offer a new Pastor in this book is to learn your church, learn your ministry, know your responsibilities, and know what is expected of you. Finally, know what you personally

Commentary for the new Pastor

believe regarding your Salvation and Church Doctrine as you serve the people of God through the *gift* of pastoring.

> *As Solomon said unto God in the late night watch when given an open forum to make his request to God, so should we say: 1 King 3:5–9 (v. 9) Give therefore thy servant an understanding heart to judge thy people, that I may discern between good and bad: for who is able to judge this, thy so great a people. This should also be your prayer for your ministry.*

Pastoral Acknowledgements

The late *Pastor Edgar Lee Jr.*: who licensed and ordained me into ministry, even allowed me to teach discipleship class as a young minister.

The late Reverend John J. Jones: when the two of us met, there were two generations that stood between us, yet our spirits bonded. You accepted us as family, my wife as your daughter, me as your son and for this I am grateful. Thank you for showing me that there is always a need for a seasoned man to be in the life of a young man.

Pastor James Bracey Sr.: for all the opportunities you gave me to preach, when no one else would; for the advice you gave me about preaching—for if I take Jesus to the grave—"I got ta," get him up.

Pastor Isaac Fletcher: there is only one of you. Thank you for the youth revivals, Friday night engagements, the long talks on the phone and even calling me your son. The most humbling act

Commentary for the new Pastor

of kindness that you've made toward me was when you retired after Pastor for thirty-two years; then you came and united with my ministry and me. Thank you.

Pastor Silas Overstreet: I will never forget the phone calls I made to you during the first year of my first pastorate, your words of advice made things easier to bear.

Pastor T. Dewitt Smith: you will never know the impact of our meetings and phone conversations in my life. Your wisdom is priceless, as the readers will discover at the conclusion of the book. Thank you for always being receptive to my telephone calls, both morning and evening.

Pastor Luther C. Cooper: the time you took to share with me and the humbleness you have always displayed made me appreciate you more, you are awesome.

Bishop Alfred A. Owens Jr. and Co-Pastor Susie Owens: Words can never express how I am so grateful for the two of you allowing my family and I and our ministry into your lives during the hour when I needed a Spiritual Father. I shall cherish this forever, because you didn't have to welcome us so warmly. Thank you for receiving me as your son in the ministry.

—*Bishop* Marc L. Neal.

Introduction

When I call to remembrance the unfeigned faith that is in thee, which dwelt first in the grandmother Lois, and thy mother Eunice; and I am persuaded that in thee also. (2 Timothy 1:6)

How this book came into existence and why

As a young boy growing up in a small to medium sized traditional Baptist church (150–200 members) in Akron, Ohio, my maternal grandparents (*William L. and Hattie Neal*) were some of the first members who served in Ministry faithfully. As children, we were brought to Sunday school and participated in Vacation Bible School, Easter programs, Youth functions and even tea and fashion shows. We, as children, were exposed to every area of the church including the cleaning of the church grounds. However, there were times while at home we discussed

Commentary for the new Pastor

various church activities and programs that were scheduled for the coming year; when they would take place, who would have what responsibility, how long it would last, what color scheme we would use, who would design which outfits, and who would be in the leading role.

Nevertheless, if there was one issue that was not discussed among us as children, it was the area regarding the business of the Church. Church business was never discussed in our presence. Before I heard anything about church business, I was well into my high school years, and before I knew or witnessed anything about church business I was on my way to college.

Basically, the only thing that we knew about church, was when Sunday came around you had to get up and get dressed, because you were going either voluntarily or by the authority and inspiration invested in Granddaddy's belt or switch. There were times when occasionally our parents would allow us to miss a Sunday service, but one thing was understood, our activities on that day were limited to what we did—except the times when we were involved in peewee football, of course our mother was a major booster parent.

As we went back and forth to Church (*The Mt. Haven Missionary Baptist Church*) there were times when I personally wondered who certain people were. Who were these distinct clubs and organizations always having bake sales, tea and fashion shows, banquets and anniversaries? Who were the special groups, which always had their announcements, read by the secretary and their flyers posted and spread across the bulletin board? Unfortunately *(maybe fortunately)* I knew nothing about church organization or structure.

Introduction

Though my father and mother as children were raised in the church *(Father-Methodist and Mother-Baptist)* and my grandparents were very instrumental in the success of the Ministry in the church; Church business, the happenings, the who, what, when, where, and whys were not shared at the dinner table nor in our presence. Certainly and strictly, Church business was just that—*Church business*.

Because church business was not discussed in our presence, that made it difficult of course for us to know whom everyone was, in particular his or her duties and responsibilities. We never knew what the deacon's purpose and function was *(other than making the little ones sit on the front pews as if they were in a boarding school)*, nor did we appreciate the janitors who served weekly cleaning up our mess within the house of God, for sure then—for pennies on the dollar.

To tell the truth, we never knew why the choir sang so loud—*(especially the same songs)*, why the Church Mothers kept mints in their purses, and why the Preacher preached so hard and melodious with his handkerchief flank behind his ear. All we knew is that we had to go to church and sit and listen for what seemed to be eight precious hours of our free time, hearing screaming on this side and hollering on that side.

Just as the Apostle Paul, who after his conversion from Saul of Tarsus wrote in 1 Corinthians 13:11, so I repeat: *When I was a child, I spake as a child, I understood as a child, but when I became a man—I put away childish things.* I now testify that the child has been put away so that the man may understand more of the mysteries and revelations of Christ and the Church.

Since becoming a Christian, the Lord has bestowed many blessings upon my family and I materialistically, seasonally, conditionally, unconditionally, but most of all spiritually, bountifully

Commentary for the new Pastor

and permanent, even to the point of counting me faithful and inducting me into the ministry.

After preaching my initial trial sermon on October 19th, 1984, I knew Gods plan for my life, but I didn't know how it was to unfold. Yes, something's were a great mystery (since we know in part) and some things still are today. As an associate Minister of Mt. Haven Baptist Church, I had the privilege and pleasure to have been invited to many area churches for preaching engagements, even candidating for vacant churches *(churches with no senior pastor)*. Yet, even then I realized my limited knowledge of Church structure and organization, especially as it varied from church to church and city-to-city.

As an associate Minister between the years of 1984 and 1990, I had both morning and evening engagements sometimes three or four times per month (sometimes more). While going from church to church, preaching and teaching, the Lord brought certain questions, issues to my heart; for everything was unique and different from one ministry to another. But how and who was ensuring these mechanical and administrative entities were fulfilled, and what various tasks were being delegated and completed was my question.

Who was making the church decisions regarding the daily administration of church business and worship service when there was no senior pastor? Who provided the guidance and direction where there was no pastoral leadership? I often wondered, why did I as a guest have to report to the seasoned Deacon with a scratch pad or the middle age woman in the office who would tell me when it was my turn to preach and what time service would normally conclude?

Then the big question for me was, when a Senior Pastor was secured, who would then be responsible for the church business;

Introduction

what happened next? After all, others had assumed the authority of the Pastor, even if only temporarily. I often pondered if the same deacon, who desired to keep his authority, would continue to tell the preacher when it was the appropriate time to preach, would the seasoned mother relinquish her *(self-appointed)* power or continue to let others know what she thought, after all she had been there 47 1/2 years. *(Think about that as I describe my first hands on experience)*

Upon the call to my first pastorate the summer of 1990 *(Second Baptist Church, Lorain, Ohio)*, I walked in ready to preach every Sunday morning, but the question in my mind was still—who did what, when, where, why, how and for what length of time? God only knew why one Deacon sat week in and week out with his arms folded and eyes half closed; while another Deacon came in late and acted as if he'd been there all the time, while another Deacon you would only see at offering time and the final Deacon when there were no sporting events to watch or play. Actually, I even wanted to know why these two ladies were always together, tighter than two peas in the pod; and why was another group so anxious to leave just as soon as service was over. Why? I didn't know but I sure wish I did as time went on.

As time progressed on, at age twenty-eight pastoring Lorain County's oldest African-American Church *(92 years in 1990)* for the first four to six months as I stuck to just preaching, there was information slipping past me that should not have. How extreme of me to think I would be kept abreast.

There were issues that I as a pastor should have been addressing instead of the trustees. There were decisions I should have been involved with and or making instead of the deacons. There was mail I should have received and opened instead of the

Commentary for the new Pastor

secretaries. There were people I should have spoken to instead of the ushers and church members. There was church property I should have known about with in the first 6 months of my assignment instead of the last 6 months of my tenure. Yet, no one told me my full responsibilities as a new pastor according to that churches doctrine and practice, only what some expected me to do other than to just preach. To simply just preach, as some would have it would be totally unbiblical; especially when you read Acts 20:28.

There in that particular passage is where the great physician Luke tells us, it is the Elder/Pastor who has been made the overseer of the church of God by the Holy Ghost to administrate as inspired. If then the Holy Ghost and not the pulpit committee, the long time church member, or the little granny in the back who slipped every Pastor a $20.00 bill hath made me the overseer, then they must oversee the church where they have been called or appointed.

> *Note: To oversee is defined as the responsibility to: supervise, manage, run, watch over, keep an eye on, administer and direct. So then an Overseer or in the Greek language— Episkopos, is one who has been charged to watch over and exercise the oversight of another in his care.*

These are all terms in which those who have been *"running"* the church in the absence of a pastor will not implore or desire to hear. *As a free point*—neither do some of the current church members who now have gone about to establish their own way of righteousness, since the arrival of the new pastor. To make a small acknowledgment, nor did the Deacons and some of the church members at my first church, especially since the church

Introduction

had been without a Senior pastor for over 18 months, and only one associate minister for the past twelve months.

Yet, know this that every Pastor should oversee the church in business, spiritually, materialistically and physically. The pastor should not just feed the flock through preaching but also administrate. Appreciate this fact, that in order to feed the flock, *(which is more than simply preaching)*, you have to know what the flock has already eaten and digested, who they are and where they've been, with whom they have eaten with and where the food has been coming from. As Pastor, you can only know this information by properly overseeing the flock, which God has placed you over.

And remember: to whom much is given, much is required.
(Luke 12:48)

Fortunately for me, after about a year or so, I began to understand Pastoring better than I did upon my arrival and I realized that it was not just typical Sunday morning preaching and going home. Then I began to do some inquiring and investigation of certain situations, positions and movements of the people, which made my first pastorate a great experience.

To the God sent or member called pastor, whether this is your very first pastorate, your second pastorate or you simply feel as though you just need to rekindle your zeal, there is pertinent information outlined through out the remaining chapters that will prayerfully prick your thoughts, shed light or confirmation upon various issues you've pondered and finally bring into focus reasoning behind a lot of unexplained church business and activities while encouraging your walk in your ministry.

Commentary for the new Pastor

The main goal in this book is to explain from a Pastoral perspective what issues and concerns you should look for and what questions to ask upon your arrival to a new appointment of Ministry or even to reaffirm your current position. My perception is that it is never too late to set the house of God in order *(Paul's advice to Timothy, 1 Timothy 3:15 and his advise to Titus, Titus 1:5)* regardless to what has previously or currently transpired. It only becomes too late when you fail to move in the spiritual realm that God has ordained you to be in, and he removes you—the candlestick, when he has commissioned you to do and to be. Keep in the forefront of your mind, you are the Pastor, not the *sheepdog* or *hireling*; you are the Pastor not a *deacon* or a *trustee*, you are the pastor and not the *policeman* or *attorney*, therefore, pastor the people of God as God instructs you.

It is God who hath given his people pastors after his own heart, to feed them with knowledge and understanding, (Jeremiah 3:15)

The Definition of the Term Church And Its Types

Unto the church of God which is at Corinth, to them that are sanctified in Christ Jesus, called to be saints, with all that in every place call upon the name of Jesus Christ our Lord, both theirs and ours: (1 Corinthians 1:2)

Actually, who is the church anyway?

Understanding the structure of the Church and how the administration functions according to the unadulterated word of God only becomes a reality when we have properly interpreted and defined the term Church. A person cannot properly oversee an organization or a group of parishioners that they do not clearly understand or know. Therefore, to pastor the church where you are, it is wise to know who the church is and also to become privy to who is the head of the church.

Commentary for the new Pastor

Definition of the word Church

The definition of the term church originated from the Greek word Ecclesia/Ekklesia, never referring to a place of worship but—translated as a called out local/universal group, separated from another by a higher authority than those who are the called. The definition in essence appears over 115 times in the Old and New Testament scriptures referencing a local company of Christians who regularly meet for religious services and to transact any and all necessary business for the proper functioning of the local church assembly.

Surprisingly enough, in our society there are still a number of individuals and multiple religious groups who continue to insist that the church is: four masonry stucco walls, an arched or pitched shingled roof, and a elaborate door on the corner of Main and Market Street, with a silver and glass beveled chandler hanging from the center of the sanctuary. Those individuals and or groups, which consistently sustain this fallible statement, should realize that the physical building is simply the meeting place for the Church *(the body of believers)* to collectively assemble to worship God our creator, which then is called the local church.

> *Note: Please be careful, for there are many local and storefront religious buildings, springing up everyday and overnight, sometimes right next door to an existing Church worship building; having a form of true godliness but really denying the authentic power thereof, from such we should turn away. Every Pastor must know the difference between a church building and a religious institution.*

Commentary for the new Pastor

Through searching of the scriptures both in the Old and New Testament, unfortunately we understand where the word *Church* does not appear in the bible until St. Matthew 16:18 in the New Testament. In this particular passage of scripture, Christ responds to the statement that Peter makes referencing Christ's identity. He says, upon this rock I will build my Church and the gates of hell shall not prevail against it (Matthew 16:18). Though the word *Church* is not mentioned until now, we can however clearly see that there is a Church *(a called out group or congregation)* in the Old Testament. There is a church without walls, a roof or an elaborate vestibule *(Exodus 5:1–19, Deuteronomy 5:22)*. This is a called-out group and is considered as the local church assembly in the wilderness that belongs to God. This "*church*" without merit given to denominationalism, religion, and hair splitting opinions and theories who in turn assembled daily and weekly for the sole purpose of worshiping the only creator—Jehovah God.

In the New Testament we can see the local church more visibly, first with the disciples that Christ called out from the world and appointed to the actual birth of the church, as it is commonly known, on the day of Pentecost. This was the celebration/feast when the disciples and others were in the upper room *(including women)* waiting for the endowment of the Holy Spirit (Acts 2). From this particular mark we see the church being more noticeable in each community of the bible. Examples to consider are the believers who were first called Christians while in Antioch *(Acts 11:26 And when he had found him, he brought him unto Antioch. And it came to pass, that a whole year they assembled themselves with the church, and taught much people. And the disciples were called Christians first in Antioch)*, and the Churches that Paul established

Commentary for the new Pastor

evangelized and wrote to, representing the local churches that served those Christians residing near those areas. Namely:

- The book of Romans to the called out Christians in the city of Rome, (Romans 1:7)
- The book of Corinthians to the called out Christians in the city of Corinth, (1 Corinthians 1:2)
- The book of Galatians to the called out Christians in the Region of Galatia, (Galatians 1:2) and so it is with the books of Thessalonians, (1 Thessalonians 1:1) Ephesians, (Ephesians 1:1) Colossians, (Colossians 1:2) and Philippians (Philippians 1:1).

Because of this advancement in ministry, we have progressed to where we are now with various and multiple types of local churches, supposedly in existence to glorify God and to minister to the immediate community in which that local church exists. So contemporarily speaking, we have the Mt. Zion's, True Light's, Shiloh's, Wilson Temples' or Second Street Tabernacle Churches etc, whether they are located in the urban city, rural township, or suburban areas.

It is also to my belief that as there are local churches we also have the Universal church. The Universal church is the spiritual church, which consists of all believers/followers of Christ. They are the sinners—who have believed and confessed in the Death, Burial, and Resurrection of Jesus Christ—*globally*. God has accepted them regardless of their race, geographical location, skin pigmentation or denomination, which in essence cannot be confined to simple walls, split-face brick and colored mortar. Christ even told his disciples; ye shall be witnesses of me first in Jerusalem, Judea, and Samaria and then to the uttermost part of

The Definition of the Term Church And Its Types

the world (Acts 1:8). This was confirming that he has established a Global or Universal church.

> Appreciate the growing fact: the Universal Church does have local Methodist, Church of God in Christ, Baptist, Pentecostal, Apostolic, Assembly of God, Church of God, Disciples of Christ and non-Denominationalist, to name a few as members—where Jesus Christ is the Chief Shepherd.

On another occasion, Jesus also told his disciples, other sheep that I have, which are not of this fold, them also I must bring in, (John 10:16) even engraft into the body of Christ.

Therefore, it is my recommendation that a newly elected and appointed Pastor never become so naive to pre-suppose that only certain denominations, religious groups, or sects of people are going to enter the Kingdom of God. You and I may have high-quality worship services, a dynamic praise and worship team, and a powerful mourners bench; yet know that God has not started calling and accepting people into the Kingdom of God with your or my particular denomination. I personally did not want to be the bearer of troublesome news but the Kingdom of God is much larger than you and I where we serve. Even if you and I are soon to be responsible for a Region, District, or State in ministry or convention, the church is still larger than us.

The Universal Church is just that *Universal*. It encompasses the Saints of God from Gintur, India to Peru, South America to Pampanga, Philippines and to the unnamed, undiscovered islands of the world. It is not limited to language, physical statue, and charismatic per sauna, economic status, seminary training, and conference affiliation or convocation attendance. Nor is it predicated upon who is voted in and voted out of the local

Commentary for the new Pastor

church. The Universal Church has Christ as the head and those called out *(the church)* as his bride, which includes others who may serve in spiritual leadership positions of the local church. Who in turn are called:

1. the body of Christ, 1 Corinthians 10:16, Ephesians 4:12,
2. the branches, St. John 15:1–10,
3. the Ambassadors of Christ, 2 Corinthians 5:20,
4. the Church of God, Acts 20:28, 1 Corinthians 1:2,
5. the Church of the Living God, 1 Timothy 3:15,
6. the Household of faith, Galatians 6:10,
7. and the Flock of God, 1 Peter 2:9.

Again, when Christ spoke to Peter and said upon this rock, I will build my church and the gates of hell shall not prevail against it *(Matthew 16:18)*, it is with the understanding that he is referencing the Universal church and not a particular local gathering of believers. If that were the case, could you imagine the denominational and spiritual chaos, the dissension and who would attempt to lay claim to whom the *real* church would be? To be honest, we have a lot of groups proclaiming and vying to be the only true way of salvation as it is now.

This is why I personally believe that the hour has drawn nigh for all Christians regardless of where they reside to consider their fellow Christian brothers and sisters, remembering them in prayer, for we are all the body of Christ. Yes it is true, we are all one body in Christ, and it becomes our responsibility to denounce

The Definition of the Term Church And Its Types

any and all schism or rupture in the body of Christ, and boldly contend for the faith in Jesus our Lord.

> *For the body is one and hath many members, and all the members of that one body, being many, are one body: so also is Christ. (1 Corinthians 12:12, KJV)*

> *Our bodies have many parts, but the many parts make up only one body when they are all put together. So it is with the "body" of Christ. (1 Corinthians 12:12, TLB)*

> *For there is but one Lord, one Faith and One Baptism, One God and father who is above all, through all and in you all. (Ephesians 4:5–6)*

So then, allow us to conclude that there is only one Church revealed *(poured as a picture of water into many glasses, the same water, but different glasses)* into many local assemblies throughout the entire world for the glorification of God, the edification of all believers, but most of all for the drawing of the unsaved to Christ. It now becomes the responsibility of each local pastor to take heed to how they oversee the ministry and people of God.

Did God Send You, or Did the Members Call You?

But the LORD said unto me, Say not, I am a child: for thou shalt go to all that I shall send thee, and whatsoever I command thee thou shalt speak. (Jeremiah 1:7)

IF YOU DON'T KNOW, THEN WHO DOES?

Qualified Pastors are constantly in demand. However, before a man or a woman can answer this question regarding their presence at a particular local Church or Assembly, the first question which must be answered, is in reference to their personal call into ministry. It will always be a mystery to a man or woman to know if they have been sent to a local church to pastor or even if they have been called by God, if they are unsure of their personal call in to the preaching, pastoring, evangelistic ministry of Christ. Every "Preacher" or prognosticator of the Gospel should unequivocally be able to clearly recite their call or acceptance

Commentary for the new Pastor

to the call of their ministry. The statements: *"I just know that he called me"*, *"my grandparents always said I would preach one day"*, *"I was down and out and had nowhere else to turn"*, should never be made by a person who believes that God has divinely called them into ministry. There should be specific events stated and quoted by each person who is in Ministry regarding their own call to be authoritative, sacrificial, competent, and successful as a pastor.

A person knowing that they have been called by God and given evidence of God's calling them from the beginning will be detrimental when considering other areas of ministry where heeding the voice of God is vitally imperative. It is my opinion that if a person is having a difficult time deciphering their personal call into ministry, they will also experience great and unique challenges when actually participating as a leader and pastor of the people of God in Ministry. Real pastoring will be birthed out of a person character, personality, and personal relationship with God.

Also, permit me to state, that I know that every pastor is not *"called or summoned"* from God into ministry, from the same method nor will they encounter the identical experiences to affirm their ministry. Everyone will not receive a burning bush experience, nor have three persons appearing unto them in the heat of the day. Neither will they dream of a ladder with angels ascending and descending in the middle of the night, nor be able to describe fire being closed up within their bones, or even recognize a brilliant light shining from heaven. For many who have been summoned into the ministry, it may appear to be as a simple as tugging on the end of your fishing line—but this time you are the fish that was unable to elude the fisherman. Yet, the most important issue to concern yourself with is not so much

Commentary for the new Pastor

how you were drawn into the gospel ministry, as it is in knowing whom the person is that has done the calling or fishing. Take into consideration; it is through different procedures that God reveals himself to man, but by the same spirit. However a person in ministry needs to know that it is God that has lured, sent for, and gestured them to herald the message of Christ and not the voice of Grandma-past.

> Note: It is every Minister's as well as Pastor's responsibility to know that God is not always in the strong wind, the earthquake, or the fire, but oftentimes he is the still small voice. (I Kings 19:11–12)

I have discovered that many *so-called* Pastors, Ministers, Evangelists, and Missionaries across the Country who are serving in these divinely appointed positions are suffering from what I term the *"Unsaved Samuel syndrome."* The Unsaved Samuel syndrome is when Samuel as a child ministered unto the Lord before Eli the Priest, and one night when he was laid down to sleep, the LORD called unto Samuel and he answered, "here am I". He ran to Eli the High Priest supposing that he had called him—*but* it was the LORD. This call transpired on two occasions, each time Eli the High Priest contradicted that he had called him, because Samuel was listening in the flesh with his natural ear and not with his spirit—he *missed* the mark. Now the key scripture and verse to consider is, 1 Samuel 3:7 where it says: Now Samuel did not yet know the LORD, neither was the word of the LORD yet revealed unto him. Viewing this scripture from a *"called"* perspective, describes for me the possibility of men and women ministering before the LORD, in the Sanctuary of the LORD, in the presence of the LORD, blessing the people of the LORD, and

Commentary for the new Pastor

yet they themselves do not personally know the LORD. Listen, you or someone you know may be gifted and talented, may have attended higher schools of learning for seminary training, hold many degrees in education or theology, and still not yet know the LORD personally. Having a sophisticated countenance or an extraordinary physique, mixed with an overtone of melodious keys doesn't qualify a man or woman to be the spiritual leader of the people of God. You may still not know God and who he is in the personal sense. It takes more than external flare, stage charisma, classroom intellect, and a fashionable countenance to know and obey God. It mandates an honorable relationship with God, the power to influence people to Christ, all incorporated with the purpose of God in order to fulfill God's predetermined will and plan.

> Note: Attending seminary schools or studying Theology is only the place of learning, not the place of calling. Understand that a person can only play with a firebomb for so long, and eventually they will get burned.

The call place for ministry always begins in your heart.

Yet, Samuel heard a voice *(perception)*, he responded to the voice *(reaction)*, but he ran unto the wrong person *(error)*. He ran to man, instead of God—*the person calling him*. Remember, previously he was unable to distinguish the voice of God from the voice of man for his lack of spiritual encountering of God. His only area of spiritual involvement for Kingdom ministry was with Eli the High Priest. Notice, when you read in verse eight of the same chapter, you will detect where it was Eli the High Priest who was responsible for providing him the necessary spiritual guidance

Commentary for the new Pastor

to hear from God, and he soon became dependant upon Eli to supply him with his spiritual substance he craved. In layman's terms, it took someone else's perception that God had summoned him to ministry. No *"Preacher"* should be so insensitive to the powerful voice of God that they hear the carnal, the flesh of man, but not the spirit of the living God. There is a danger in solely hearing and reacting to the voice of man in the infant stages of a Pastorate. Historically, these will cause a person to manufacture what they hear in the flesh, into the spiritual voice of God later in Ministry, especially if they fail to mature rapidly. Every Man and Woman of God should know at the time of their calling and appointment, as Samuel did later in verse 19 of Chapter 3, that the LORD was with him. You need to know this early in ministry. If you don't know this, then who will know? Who called Samuel? It was God that called and sent him to minister—not man. You must know who called and mandated you to set at liberty those who are bound to preach the acceptable year of the Lord and the recovery of sight to those who are spiritually blind.

> Note: If you fail to perceive that God is with you at the inception of your ministry, what is ahead will naturally become an experience of unnecessary turmoil, frustration and chaos. If you never know if the Deacons or Elders are with you, you need the blessed assurance that Jehovah God is on your side.

After conferring with many Pastors globally, it has been agreed upon that every Minister going into the Pastoralship should know if God sent him or her to Pastor in California, New York, Texas, or even to stay where they are and help cultivate that particular ministry. Too many ministers have vacated a particular ministry in hopes of becoming the senior pastor, when God has

Commentary for the new Pastor

not authorized their exodus or confirmed their relocation. Each minister should know if God commissioned him or her to lead a ministry with an administrative or charismatic approach or if they are simply moving in the realm of self and/or their higher education and resume flare. Not knowing this is absolutely unacceptable and dangerous. To the prospective Pastor, do you know where God has actually called and sent you to minister? Hypothetically, did God send you *Saul*, to Israel or did the people want and desire a King to be like the other nations so intensely that they rushed God and ignored his leading? Now permit me to ask, did God send you *David* to Israel, because you were the chosen King for that particular sect of people, or did the people simply settle for you because God reject their desired King?

If I could say it another way, are you presently serving in a position of ministry because the people were so desperate to be as other churches and you so desperately wanted to pastor a church, that you accepted the first opportunity to simply change your environment? Or did the church wait on God to send you to them and did you wait on God to send you to them? News flash, just because the members or the presiding-prelate of the Church where you are currently serving or crave to be, voted for you, desired you, sponsored an installation service for you, and now feel as though you are for them; understand spiritually, this may not be what or where God has predestined for your future. It could be your in-between state and you are trying to make it your dream home. Don't become so spiritually blind and narrow-minded that you fail to see God in your future, because you are too consumed by your past and even present conditions.

Every Minister and Pastor must learn the dynamics of pastoring and quickly yearn to see God for their self, instead of accepting how people compose and construct God to appear

Commentary for the new Pastor

before them. As an eye opener, you and I could readily end up Pastoring the people of God when God has not ordained us to, simply because there appears to be an opportunity, and the people are going more by a vote in a business meeting than a tugging within the spirit. You and I could purposely stumble into what God has predestinated to be the end of your beginning in Ministry. So now the question is, did God send you or did the members call you? If you cannot answer that, then moving through the next few chapters for application will be as difficult as a mosquito winning a war against an alligator.

How can they preach, accept they be sent? (Romans 10:15)

Notice the call procedure, God initially calls the man or woman into ministry for a specific purpose and then commissions that person to an identifiable people with his exclusive authority and not mans. He also charges them with the relevant purpose to be fulfilled in the lives of the particular people; while he or she continues to experience and realize more of the presence of God. The sent Pastor will experience more of God, especially when they have been sent by God to pour and invest into the lives of God's people—because God is continuing to pour into them. If a pastor attempts to lead, guide, direct, shepherd, nurture, protect, or even water and feed the members of a local assembly without the insignia of the Chief Shepherd, that ministry will almost immediately become more draining than joyous, and more burdensome than blissful for the called pastor. This is because he or she is emptying themselves into the lives of those that they are Pastoring, but never personally being rejuvenated and refreshed themselves. Stand firm on the principal—if God sent you, he will always refresh, recharge, and restore you for serving and

Commentary for the new Pastor

ministering to His people. The more you make yourself available for service the more frequent you will measure and sense your personal growth into ministry.

Notice the specific people called, and their specific audience

- God called Noah to preach for 120 years concerning the flood that was to come
- God called Moses to preach deliverance to the Israelites while in the land of Egypt
- God called Jeremiah to preach the acceptable year of the Lord to the people of Judah
- God called Isaiah to remind Israel of their desolate city
- God called Jonah to prophesy unto the nation of Nineveh
- God called Joshua to lead Israel into the promise land;
- Finally, what has God specifically called you to do and where has he purposely sent you, knowing— the steps of a good man are ordered by the Lord (Psalms 37:23)?

Words of Wisdom

Regardless if a ministry does call you to pastor, it is recommended by many pastors that you should not accept the position of Pastoring if God has not ordained the union, *for it is a marriage*. Accept the fact, that everyone in ministry is not called to be a pastor or to pastor a local assembly though he or she is in ministry. Some ministers simply sense a spirit of zealousness and vile fragrance of egotism motivated out of their own heart and not

Commentary for the new Pastor

because God established it. Please know for yourself if Jehovah God has enlisted you into pastoral ministry and deployed you on to your battlefield, to pluck up, pull down, and to destroy the church enemies—*for pastoring is spiritual warfare.*

So then it is my suggestion to each Pastor receiving the pastoral reigns voluntarily or involuntarily, that they should know four relevant points regarding their call into ministry.

1. *Before God formed us in the womb, he had already preordained us for a particular area of ministry, within a certain dispensation period; and all we have to do is submit to his purpose. This may be your season, and then again it may not be—but get ready.*

2. *It is not of any merit of our own that we are where we are, God has counted us faithful, by placing us into the Ministry and therefore we have no reason to gloat in our success or ironically to be afraid of the people's faces.*

3. *Also know if you are going to be the pastor of the local assembly or if you are going to be everyone's friend. It is important to know you cannot be the pastor and friend in the common sense. Familiarity breeds contentment and loss of respect.*

4. *Each Pastor will soon learn the need to balance their ministry, family, and home even if they are bi-vocational. Don't let Satan gain the advantage and deceive you into thinking you have time to balance your family and home and this feat is simply of no great concern.*

Now an additional thought regarding your call into ministry is, the more intimate and sensitive a pastor develops his or her level of spiritual perception to the voice of God, the greater the

Commentary for the new Pastor

opportunity it will be for one to distinguish the voice of God from himself or anyone else, including other church and family members *(who may be spiritual)*. Not knowing if God has birthed ministry into your spirit is as dangerous as a married woman giving birth to another man's baby, sadistically massaging your own ego, or committing spiritual masturbation. It is my strong opinion, if God the Holy Spirit has not birthed ministry into your spirit you need to know who did and then make some serious adjustments regarding your ministry. Hypothetically, if one of your Grandparents ironically birthed ministry into you, then metaphorically you are impregnated with your Grandparents child *(vision for you)*, if you have allowed one of your siblings to pour their vision for you into you, then you are symbolically committing spiritual incest, or if you conjured ministry within yourself, then you are schizophrenically in quest of self-gratification.

Pastoring is an endowment from God; not an opportunity to seek self-satisfaction or elevation for ones' self-image or relative. As a man or woman of God no one should see more within you and your life than what you see in you through the eyes of the Holy Spirit. Learn to look at your own situation, take notice to what it will become, more so than what it currently exist as, know where you are and where God desires for you to be. If you are not there yet, don't panic gently begin moving in that direction immediately to fulfill the purpose of God in your life. Yes, God does have a plan for you, because God has you on his mind (Jeremiah 29:11, for God knows the thoughts that he thinks toward us) if you will only distinguish who ushered you to the location where you are currently serving, and not be ashamed.

If you are unsure if God has sent you to the ministry where you are or if the members were the voice you took heed to, don't

Commentary for the new Pastor

advance any further, close the book now. For in the following chapters you will discover topics that I believe that should be considered and addressed in every new pastorate by the Pastor who has now began his or her ministry. In the following chapters, there rest layers of information readily and available to aid you and your ministry. Now that you are there, what's next? If you don't know how you arrived at this particular pastorate, then the message that is shared from your lips to the member's ears, from your heart to their spirit will be blurred and misconstrued at best. Take the necessary time to reacquaint yourself with your own personal call into ministry as a plight to do the will of God.

CHAPTER ONE

The Doctrinal Statement

As I besought thee to abide still at Ephesus, when I went into Macedonia, that thou mightest charge some that they teach no other doctrine, Neither give heed to fables and endless genealogies, which minister questions, rather than godly edifying which is in faith: *so do.* (1 Timothy 1:3–4)

KNOW WHAT YOU BELIEVE AND STAND ON IT

*N*ow that we have been able to discern between the local Assembly of Believers, the Universal Church of God, and your call into Ministry allow us now to progress inside of the concrete and masonry walls, under the pitched roof, through the oak, and glass stained doors of the local church and ask some basic questions—that will prayerfully be answered.

Commentary for the new Pastor

First, from a general perspective, what do you know about this particular church when you first walked in to be a member or as a pastorial candidate, who did you know, and what did you know upon your arrival? What did you know about that church and church in general? Let us get a little personal, why did you choose that particular ministry to be associated with or desire to become Pastor of from the beginning,

- because of the churches popularity / notoriety
- because your Grandfather, Father or Uncle was the founder
- because you inherited it upon your relative's demise
- because your ministerial clock was and is fading *(and you hurriedly took the first church calling)*
- Or, is it because you believe that God in his infinite wisdom created that particular opportunity especially for you? Why are *you* there? *Remember every Minister who knew of the vacancy of the church, also prayed and asked God for special consideration,* but why are *you* there?

These questions are necessary for discussion and worthy of an answer as a person decides and ponders to lead a particular ministry or to be affiliated with a significant congregation. What is seen with the natural eye of man may not always be what presides over a local church on the inside, especially spiritually. In order to see within a churches ministry you cannot glance past the church from a carnal or natural perspective, the church is spiritually discerned.

The Doctrinal Statement

But the natural man receiveth not the things of the Spirit of God: for they are foolishness unto him: neither can he know them, because they are spiritually discerned. (1 Corinthians 2:14 KJV)

The man without the Spirit does not accept the things that come from the Spirit of God, for they are foolishness to him, and he cannot understand them, because they are spiritually discerned. (1 Corinthians 2:14 NIV)

Let us be honest with one another, there may be nice church members at the local church you are candidating for or have been recently called to, the decorum may be corresponding from the vestibule to the baptistery, and the choir(s) may be *"jammin"* to the hilt, but the question still remains what and who governs the church administratively where you are or covet to be? There has to be a foundation sound in doctrine covering the people of God and a firm structure supporting the house of God from the weight of society.

As a New pastor, the first particular area of concern for any Pastor to reference should have been the church Doctrinal Statement or Articles of faith. This query should occur prior to your move into the churches parsonage, before you hire a Minister of Music, before you consider who to move out of office and who to keep in office. Too often these important documents are excluded from any interview or consultation, from any area of investigation, or priority checklist when a new Minister takes hold of the church's helm. It is true that many times it is an oversight stemming from the new pastor's zealousness to be and not his or her spiritual discernment to discover; yet somebody needs to stop and ponder it in detail. Generally, we as a people don't become immediately concerned about this area until once

Commentary for the new Pastor

they are officially elected into office, then if we sense that the Doctrinal Statement is not what we thought that it would be, then we become enthused to modify it.

> Notice: this is an inappropriate perception and a task that will not be easily achieved.

From the preliminary interview, the simple question should blatantly be asked, what does that particular church believe and practice? (As the council has prepared a list of questions for you, you must also arrive prepared to question the committee). I must inform and caution you, do not become impressed by the Church name, whether it is Baptist, Methodist, Pentecostal, Church of God in Christ, Lutheran, Apostolic or Catholic. The title adjacent to the local name, whether it is *Sweetwater Holy Ghost Baptist church, St. Paul the Episcopal Fire Baptized A.M.E.Z., House of prayer for all people Non-Denomination or J.C. Sample's Temple Church of God in Christ*—doesn't make it a Church. The name doesn't automatically or theoretically suggests or indicate that they believe and accept the total inerrant Word of God through Jesus Christ as the only means of Salvation.

> *Neither is there salvation in any other: for there is none other name under heaven given among men, whereby we must be saved. (Acts 4:12 KJV)*

> *Salvation is found in no one else, for there is no other name under heaven given to men by which we must be saved. (Acts 4:12 NIV)*

It would be in a Pastor's best interest prior to committing to or accepting any position of spiritual leadership to read and re-read

The Doctrinal Statement

the doctrinal and article of faith statement that the church is supposedly built upon. For other foundation can no man lay than that is laid, which is Jesus Christ (1 Corinthians 3:11). Don't be too insecure or overly confident to ask someone who knows what are the foundation for Worship, for Government, for Discipline, and their authority. Ask them, what do they believe and practice with regards to Salvation, the Holy Spirit, Redemption, the Blood of Christ, the Virgin Birth, Holiness, Sin, and its consequences. If you really want to throw them for a loop, *(and possibly squash your pastoral chances)* ask them their theological belief and position in regards to Tongue speaking, the interpretation of Tongues, and also Women sharing in Ministry.

It is evident that the discussion of true and false doctrine has always been a concern in the church; notice the scripture when certain brothers promoted circumcision and Paul and Barnabas had to go up to Jerusalem for clarity and reinforcement. As a common expression—someone needed to be straightened out theologically.

> *And certain men which came down from Judea taught the brethren, and said, Except ye be circumcised after the manner of Moses, ye cannot be saved. When therefore Paul and Barnabas had no small dissension and disputation with them, they determined that Paul and Barnabas, and certain other of them, should go up to Jerusalem unto the apostles and elders about this question. (Acts 15:1–2)*

Be very direct and sure when you ask the committee and/or church officers what they believe, that you know what you believe, and have been persuaded in your own mind. Don't ever assume that just because you arrive at a particular ministry and they profess to be devoted to you and your family that they

Commentary for the new Pastor

practice strong biblical principals and are willing to condemn what is non-biblical simply because you suggest it. It may be right, but people have a tendency to rebel against change. People will blatantly defy change, especially when it affects them directly. *(Even the Apostle Peter and the Apostle Paul had a confrontation regarding doctrine—see Galatians 2:1–21).*

For a congregation to change their conduct and activities would indicate that they have been doing something unproductive and erroneous for a particular period of time while in the absence of a pastor, or for a designated period of time when a pastor was present. Just remember, typically people don't like change, unless it is addressing the conduct of other church members and not their own.

> *2 Timothy 3:7–8, Ever learning, and never able to come to the knowledge of the truth. Now as Jannes and Jambres withstood Moses, so do these also resist the truth: men of corrupt minds, reprobate concerning the faith*—KJV

> *2 Timothy 3:7–8, always learning but never able to acknowledge the truth. Just as Jannes and Jambres opposed Moses, so also these men oppose the truth—men of depraved minds, who, as far as the faith is concerned, are rejected*—NIV.

While discussing and reviewing the church's doctrinal statement or articles of faith, there are some general points of concern to take into consideration and hold true to, even if it means you're not accepting the position of leadership. You have to know what you believe. Not knowing what you believe can cause another to insinuate that their doctrine is true and acceptable to you and your practicing belief.

The Doctrinal Statement

Doctrinal Statement

The church doctrinal statement is the canon or standard that all members have adopted as their spiritual and moral code of ethics. It has become the paradigm for which each person, publicly and privately, have acknowledged as the plane to which their lives will be spiritually governed. It unmistakably describes who they *(the church members)* believe to be their Savior, Messiah, Deliverer, and the only means of salvation. After reading this particular paricape there should be no question or reservation to whom faith is put in.

A person who reads the Church doctrinal statement should see Redemption very clearly via their Savior *(who by the way should be Jesus the Christ)*. Anyone examining this document should discover strong evidence referencing the Forgiveness of Sin, the Freeness of Salvation, the purpose of the Holy Spirit, Church rule, or government, marks of our Adversary the Devil, Justification, even our Sanctification, the Fall of man, Stewardship and Tithing, the return of Christ, and Baptismal and Communion. There should be biblical explanations with scriptural support for each article listed. If a church is unable to produce a solid doctrinal statement with scripture to support their belief *(and correct interpretation)*, then the potential minister should be very sensitive and concerned to what has been the spiritual foundation for that particular ministry historically.

If there are questions regarding the spiritual beliefs of a church, during the interview process is when many questions should be asked and addressed. Believe me when I tell you, some people *(even those in leadership)* may not know what the church, as a whole believes in concerning their Theology. To be candid, many church members will Isogisis—*read into a*

Commentary for the new Pastor

particular passage of scripture, instead of Exogisis—*receive out of the scriptures* exactly what is being offered. For some churches, doctrinal statements are as old as *dirt* itself, but because they have been deeply imbedded into the history and archives of the church everyone generally assumes that it is correct rather than researching it and knowing factually.

Other guides to Church Doctrinal Statements

Included with the Church Doctrinal statement there should be a church Constitution, or to use the "B" word the Bylaws. A church Constitution or the Bylaws must first be understood as being a research tool for those individuals who boldly and clearly choose to consciously disregard what the Word of God has previously established for the church as a form of government, organizational leadership, and structure.

God's word has already defined each position in the church and their authority, even how the church members should conduct themselves *(Hebrews 13:17, 1 Timothy 3:14– 16)*. Nevertheless, from time to time there tends to be church members who would rather consult their own personal manuals or selected material to bring into their meetings or even recommend for the church business meetings if allowed. Because of this, there lies the church constitution or bylaws exhibiting the church's leadership and their duties, qualifications and means for appointment along with their term to hold office.

It is true that various rules and regulations will apply or differ from denomination to denomination, yet all the rules and guidelines stating the procedures should always be so mention in accordance to the inerrant word of God. Most churches in conjunction with the word of God have adopted other pieces of material to support their structure. Some of the material includes,

The Doctrinal Statement

Robert Rules of Order, Hiscox Baptist Directory—but be careful of those who still implement Mason practices, Eastern Star rules, Union and Steward principals from their place of employment also known as, United Rubber or Steel Workers Union. It should be clearly noted that if these pieces of material are selected to be part of the Churches Constitution *(may God have mercy)*, all should then note that *nothing, I said nothing, nothing,* supersedes or compares with the inerrant written Word of God.

The church constitution should not be adjusted or be curtailed to fit a certain person's lifestyle to give them the immoral freedom of their choice. As a matter of fact, nothing should be contained in the Constitution or adopted from, nor supported manual that goes against or questions the Word of God. Man made guidelines or material should only serve as that—*a guide,* to assist in a particular area of ministry and organization.

While reviewing the Constitution or Bylaws it is also important to become familiar with the date *(including the month and year)* of when they were written, with the appropriate committee members names and signatures signing as a form of acknowledgment and acceptance.

> *Note: Sometimes, there are business-meeting minutes substantiating that they were read and approved in the annual or special called church meeting. Often, By-laws and or Church Constitutions are read three times before the Congregation prior to becoming authentic.*

It is pertinent for a Minister to re-evaluate this information prior to accepting a position of leadership, for two blunt and candid reasons. The first reason, the church in all probability will not change the constitution or by-laws just for you, and two it may

Commentary for the new Pastor

save you some hardship in the future if you decide to accept the position to lead the congregation anyway. To the potential pastor of the Greater Pentecostal Mt. Zion Baptist Holiness Assembly of the Church of God in Christ, know the Doctrine of the Church, where you are, and their Church Constitution. But most of all, know what *you* believe.

> *Note: If you don't know what you believe and why, you are liable to succumb to another person's theology and doctrine, which makes you their disciple and not Christ's.*

CHAPTER TWO

Church Ordinances

They shall leave none of it unto the morning, nor break any bone of it: according to all the ordinances of the passover they shall keep it. (Numbers 9:12)

WHAT HAVE YOU ACCEPTED AS BEING INSTITUTED BY CHRIST?

Considering the Church Ordinances (*statutes and traditions*) that are honored and defined as the spiritual rules and regulations of the local church, traditionally there are only two types of ordinances to be followed. There are two that most denominations generally accept and recognize as being instituted by God, through his son Jesus. Occasionally, there will be some churches that recognize three types of ordinances.

Traditionally, they are:

Commentary for the new Pastor

1) Baptism,

2) Communion (the Lord's Supper),

and where applicable depending upon the denomination and/or geographical location

3) Foot washing

It is imperative to know what is customary, ritualistic, traditional, biblical, and what is man-made. Unfortunately, many people have gone to hell or are living a life engulfed in spiritual bondage, because they have decided to hold onto the ungodly tradition, rituals, and governments made by man. Too many Christians/Believers in the power of God are choosing to die with the King Saul's of Christendom *(the old regime)* instead of living with the King David's of Christendom *(the new era)*. The church is filled with members who have chosen to live in Egypt *(with the pleasures of sin—the past—the previous administration)* than to travel through the wilderness of life to the promise land of God. To many Christians are content with being the offspring's of Ishmael—*a bondwoman's child*, instead of desiring to be the children of Isaac—*a freewoman's inheritor*. Question, why should anyone be content with being a Prince when God has already predestinated you to be a King?

The Ordinances are part of who we are, and gives us the reason why we believe

The First ordinance generally accepted is Water Baptism. Baptism comes from the Greek word Baptizo' which clearly states to be totally immersed or submerged, to dip as one would submerge a piece of clothing material into a pool of dye to change

Church Ordinances

its' color. Record for future references, that Baptism/Baptizo is not the sprinkling or splattering of water on a person's forehead, but again it is the total submersion of an individual from head to toe into water; whether it is in a gorgeous Ivory marble pool or a muddy, seaweed, bluegill infested pond.

Note: Water Baptism should only take place after a person has confessed their sins, and not in hopes of having their sins forgiven or washed clean.

We as Christians are baptized out of a converted heart to be identified with Christ's death, burial and resurrection (Romans 6). Regardless of our denomination, before we are baptized, we should have already been *"born again"* according to the washing and regeneration of the Holy Spirit— *Titus 3:5b.*

As a contemporary minister, there are very important entities that should be identified and considered in order to properly share in the sacred water baptism of the new candidate. Now, I am not going to split hairs with whose name the baptismal should be in, whether you use Acts 2:38—*Then Peter said unto them, Repent, and be baptized everyone of you in the name of Jesus Christ for the remission of sins, and ye shall receive the gift of the Holy Ghost* or Matthew 29:19–20—*Go ye therefore, and teach all nations, baptizing them in the name of the Father, and of the Son, and of the Holy Ghost: Teaching them to observe all things whatsoever I have commanded you: and, lo, I am with you always, even unto the end of the world. Amen.* For if they have not been submerged into the Spiritual body of Christ, then they are still going straight to Hell, with a one way ticket—end of story

Commentary for the new Pastor

Tidbits to know regarding a person baptism

First-know if they *(the candidate(s))* have been made fully aware to what baptism is and what baptism is not? This includes knowing the purpose of Baptism.

Secondly-do they *(the candidate (s))* have an accurate working knowledge of what they are embarking upon, or is it a cute statement being made because of their friend or relative being baptized, or even because Momma made them?

Thirdly-is it because they were recently caught in a lie or found out that they were actually going to jail or even been diagnosed with a terminal disease, and now they want to get right with God? Let us never assume that a person knows what is transpiring in the spiritual realm regardless to what their age is.

Baptismal pool location

The baptism pool(s) location is also very important to review and evaluate, never assume that every church has a pool for baptism or its location is easily accessible. Many churches in this dispensation continue to share baptism pools with other churches. In such cases agreeable arrangements are normally made with the local sister church which should be at the convenience of both covenant churches.

Baptism pools are often located in incuspicious locations, even under the sanctuary's' pulpit, while others are suitably located in the basement or appropriately behind the choir loft or pulpit area. Please never be embarrassed to ask where the Baptism pool

Church Ordinances

is, just become embarrassed if you are in one place while the candidate(s) are somewhere else.

Who fills the water in the Baptismal pool

It is also necessary to determine who is responsible for filling and draining the pool with water on or before the required day. Whoever have been appointed to care for the pool should do so with preciseness, accuracy and commitment. It is embarrassing to have a baptism scheduled and discover there is no water in the pool—*Lawd have mercy*. The day baptisms are scheduled is imperative because you do not want the water or the candidate to be too early or too late. It is embarrassing to the pastor, church, and for church members and family members to assemble in preparation for a baptismal (*our families will travel from afar for a baptismal service*) and there is not enough water in the baptismal pool, the temperature of the water is in error, or the baptismal pool water is unsanitary from the previous baptismal. As a matter fact it is upsetting for everyone if there is a low water level that is unsafe for the baptismal of the candidates—and the person has to now wait.

Though the baptismal water does not save a person nor spiritually revive him or her, take a mental note that the water should always be fresh *(for hygiene sake and sanitation purposes)*, and not left remaining from a previous baptismal service. Now if there is a heater or filter attached to the baptismal pool these also should be regularly checked and cleaned as a preventative measure. Through researching I have noticed not all churches and pastors baptize on the same day and time. Yes, some are in the AM while others are in the PM and some are on the first Sunday of each month while others are either the second, third

Commentary for the new Pastor

or forth Sunday, all at that particular Churches discretion. Don't be afraid to ask.

The Second ordinance, Communion *(Koinonia—partnership or fellowship)* or the Lords Supper—is also an ordinance that our Lord Jesus instituted for us to keep as a sacred memorial of him. The Communion elements that we partake of are identified as *1) unleavened bread*, bread that does not contain any yeast, for yeast is a representation of sin, therefore it is recommended not to use bread with yeast/nor saltine crackers as part of the Lords Supper, and *2) the fruit of the vine or unfermented wine also known as grape juice (new wine)*. It is strongly recommended that nonalcoholic grape juice or wine be used. Christ's blood was not mingled nor tainted with any foreign substance of society. Be prepared to acknowledge that the unleavened bread represents his broken body while the unfermented grapes represents Christ's shed blood on Calvary Hill, *(1 Corinthians 10:16)*.

Traditionally and respectfully, only those who are born again believers should participate in the sacraments of communion. The Lords Supper is to be kept Holy and sacred, each man, woman or child examining him or herself that he or she has not intentionally harbored sin within their heart. Pastor, it is your responsibility to make sure that you and your congregation are not becoming weak in spirit, heart, mind, and soul because your participation in communion is spiritually defiled.

> *Wherefore whosoever shall eat this bread, and drink this cup of the Lord, unworthily, shall be guilty of the body and blood of the Lord. But let a man examine himself, and so let him eat of that bread, and drink of that cup. For he that eateth and drinketh unworthily, eateth and drinketh damnation to himself, not discerning the Lord's body. For this cause many are weak and sickly among you, and many sleep (1 Corinthians 11:27–30 KJV).*

Church Ordinances

Therefore, whoever eats the bread or drinks the cup of the Lord in an unworthy manner will be guilty of sinning against the body and blood of the Lord. A man ought to examine himself before he eats of the bread and drinks of the cup. For anyone who eats and drinks without recognizing the body of the Lord eats and drinks judgment on himself, That is why man among you are weak and sick, and an umber of you have fallen asleep (1 Corinthians 11:27–30 NIV).

It is also essential and imperative to discover the policies and procedures regarding serving communion that each church uses and to know the date and times along with the frequency of communion. Let me say it loud and clear, there are no set days or times nor is it etched in the sands of time how often communion should be participated in, *just ensure that each participant observes it correctly.* There are some churches that receive communion only on the first Sunday of the month while others receive it every Sunday. The most important point for consideration is not for us to receive communion with unconfessed sin in our life—*don't give refuge to sin*—your family nor friends are not really worth you going to hell over.

As with Baptism, it is also recommended with Communion to inquire about:

a) who sets up the communion table,

b) who prepares the elements,

c) who is responsible for the cleaning of the communion trays,

d) where are the communion elements stored and most of all,

Commentary for the new Pastor

    e) who takes communion to those members who are sick and shut-in or the elderly members who are unable to commune in the worship service?

As previously stated, most churches offer Communion during their morning worship services, but there are also those who remain convinced that it is the *Lords Supper* and should be received only during the evening service. Because of their particular dogma, they will only serve and partake of the elements during that hour. Yet, all will concur that there is no particular hour that the word of God proclaims that it should be observed, just as often as ye eat and drink.

Lastly, the Third ordinance is Foot-washing. For those who believe that foot washing is an ordinance, *(traditionally it is only those of certain denominations)* it is typically observed in or at a special worship service. It is the time where those in leadership exemplify genuine humility and servanthood—and God knows we surely need that amongst our churches. Most churches observe foot-washing because of the episode recorded in St. John 13:1–15, where Christ is found washing the feet of his disciples. (There he shares with his disciples, if I then, your Lord and Master, have washed your feet; ye also ought to wash one another's feet. For I have given you an example, that ye should do as I have done to you).

Generally, foot-washing worship services are held at an appointed hour and someone is designated by the Senior Minister to have the parishioners gather in small groups and then water is ceremonially poured on the top of the foot (always from the calf muscle downward and below the ankle). This is primarily observed because it was customary in the Old Testament as well

Church Ordinances

as the New Testament, that when family or friends traveled from a great distance and upon their arrival, they would remove there shoes or sandals and the host would bath the feet of the guest as being welcomed into their home. Surely we still can benefit from this practice of humility, yet more so to being obedient unto the commandments of Christ. Church ordinances vary from denomination to denomination, your responsibility is to bring clarity to the members that hear your voice regarding why you believe and practice what you do.

CHAPTER THREE

Ministers, Evangelist, Missionaries, Associates, and Elders

And the things that thou hast heard of me among many witnesses, the same commit thou to faithful men, who shall be able to teach others also. (2 Timothy 2:2)

NOT ALL ARE QUALIFIED TO BE WHERE THEY ARE, SOME ARE CANDIDLY-WANNABES

*C*onfronting the subject matter of Associate Ministers, Evangelists, Missionaries, Elders or other leadership areas of the Church is always a delicate issue for a new pastor, regardless if you are inheriting a traditional or progressive ministry. Providing spiritual leadership to those who have been called by God can be exasperating. Becoming heir to a ministry from a retired, deceased, or technically removed pastor where ministers have been licensed and ordained under that spiritual covering will undoubtfully have it's challenges. As a matter of fact, there will be pros as well as cons, typically based upon your standard of ministry and code of

Commentary for the new Pastor

ministerial and pulpit etiquettes and requirements. This possibly will be mentally and spiritually wearisome for the relationship, in comparison to what they have previously been permitted to do and not do under the previous administration.

> Note: Tighten up your shoelaces and unloosen your tie for there are sensitive matters to be concentrated on with the Ministers, Evangelist, Elders and Missionaries that will cause you to reevaluate your acceptance to that particular Ministry. And may God help you if you are unsure or have any reservations regarding your appointment.

The foremost area of concern in my opinion is for every Assistant, Associate, Elder, Missionary, Minister or Evangelist to know their precise field or realm of ministry and function in it as they have been placed by the Senior Pastor, more so than where they desire to be. It has been many Assistants' desires—that have become the gateway for much spiritual unrest within the Churches ministry.

> Note: Even if you were negligent as an Assistant, Associate, Elder, Adjutant, Evangelist or Minister in supporting your Pastor or area of ministry you must not accept anything less than what God has established where you currently serve. It is never too late to require the standard of excellence in ministry. The cycle of the rebellious spirit must be broken.

Knowing your title and status

Every Minister, Evangelist, Missionary or even Adjutant and Assistant to the Pastor must know that they are just that, the assistant. An adjutant or assistant is one that is defined as a helper or one who provides support to the Chief, the person in

Ministers, Evangelist, Missionaries, Associates, and Elders

authority. Each assistant to the pastor must recognize and accept the fact that they are subordinate and secondary in ministerial rank and not the primary personage. Since they are not the Pastor no one should extend or request any Pastoral privileges or constitutional rights.

The Bible teaches us through the life of Moses and other leaders, that God delicately aligns assistants with His leaders. Notice when Moses was called to lead the children of Israel out of the Egyptian Bondage that Aaron was called to assist him specifically, and Joshua was appointed by God as his minister or assistant and to finally receive the rod of authority to lead Israel into the promise land (Numbers 27:18). Elijah was the prophet called of God to Minister before the people, yet Elisha had the responsibility of serving and ministering to him prior to receiving a double portion of Elijah's spirit or mantle or cloak of spiritual covering (2 Kings 2:1–25). Therefore each assistant or associate must know His or Her spiritual gifts for serving in ministry, under the covering of the Senior Pastor and that he or she can only receive what the Senior Pastor has, if they would first serve. It is true that rivers flows down stream, rain falls from the sky, that lightening strikes from the east to the west, and so it is that anointing falls from the head down. If there is not an anointed head there cannot be an anointed body. Whatever occurs within the head eventually transpires and affects the body, including the assistant ministers.

Each Pastor should hurriedly sit down and review each assistant or associate assessment and point of view on ministry and it's definition, the Pastors responsibility, their own personal goals and responsibilities and their call into ministry. Doing this within a reasonable period of time can and will (*sometimes*)

Commentary for the new Pastor

prevent discord in the future. It will also set the tone for the spirit of accountability.

> *Note: Every person must learn how to serve someone else before they are served themselves. Don't think that God will allow you to be abundantly served when you cannot humble yourself to minister to the Man or Woman of God.*
>
> *Ephesians 4:11 And he gave some, apostles; and some, prophets; and some, evangelists; and some, pastors and teachers;*

There have been many pastors who have inherited ministries where the pastor has retired or have become demised and the assistant or associate Pastor, Elder, Minister or even Evangelist subtly insinuates that they should have been considered for the vacant pastorate and not the person currently candidating or elected. They have believed so because they possibly could be long standing church members, their relative was the founder, or presiding prelate, or someone promised them. If they have been overlooked *(for whatever the reason)*, they may spew the flavor of bitter vinegar upon the ministry and the new Pastor without explanation. The best advice is to ensure that each minister knows his or her position of ministry with you and within the Church. For there will be times that you are to take them with you, and they are to share with you, but then there are times when you should leave them at home. *Know who to take and who not to take.*

What do you know about them—those in Ministry

While determining this area of Ministry, it is also beneficial to the innovative pastor to know three key elements regarding the assistants or associates. Knowing these areas will cause life and

Ministers, Evangelist, Missionaries, Associates, and Elders

ministry where you are to be more tolerable. Again, my experience has advised me to inquire of three key areas, they are:

1. Know if they are actually licensed ministers for the preaching ministry, and if so under what authority and by whom. Where did their license come from, was it a local pastor, a local church, or did it originate from an online service or mail in application. As an additional point, you want to know what was the written, doctrinal, and seminarian criteria that the potential had to fulfill in order to be an assistant or associate minister. Blatantly stated, were their any special courses or curriculums that they were mandated to study?

2. Verify if they are ordained as a Minister, Elder or Evangelist. It is again beneficial for the pastor to determine again under whose authorization and jurisdiction this has taken place. Let me also suggest that there be an inquiry of who were the council members that laid hands upon them. It would also be to your advantage to know what authority had been given to them since they are now "ordained." Finally what were the criteria for them to fulfill in order to be ordained—*was there an examination?*

3. Finally, question if they are responsible for any particular area within the ministry, for example: Bible Study, Baptismals, Counseling, Preaching, Teaching, Hospital visitation, Discipleship training, Educational department etc. If they are accountable for certain areas within the ministry, the next question is are they fulfilling the obligations entrusted unto them? But most importantly what material is being used for teaching purposes and if it has received pastoral approval.

Commentary for the new Pastor

Additional Inquiries for your staff

Other questions to require of them are, if they are married or single (and the length of time), have they attended any College, Seminary or Post-Graduate School, how long have they been affiliates with this particular ministry, have they shared in ministry with another church, why did they leave or were asked to leave, have they served in any other area of ministry prior to their acceptance to the ministry (Usher, Deacon, Choir President etc …), and any other question that you may consider asking as the Senior Pastor. It is always good to ask.

It is important to remind Ministerial Assistants and Associates that ministry is more than administrative preaching in the pulpit, or officiating of the Sunday morning worship service. Upscale and aggressive Ministry is serving the people of God and meeting the Church members' spiritual needs *(seasoned and youth members)* while keeping and fulfilling the vision of the Senior Pastor.

Therefore, we should have qualified assistance in ministry, particularly if we have these individuals amongst or on our staff:

1. Associates Ministers-generally licensed ministers

2. Evangelists-those who are licensed to exercise their gift abroad

3. Missionaries-those who are commissioned to specific areas

4. Elders-normally ordained lay ministers, often appointed pastors

5. Teachers-generally lay men and women

Ministers, Evangelist, Missionaries, Associates, and Elders

6. Pastoral Assistants-licensed, ordained and functioning in a pastoral capacity

How many Ministers are there?

An additional area of pertinence that should be considered by the Senior Pastor is knowing the number of Ministers that are currently serving as lay Ministers or the predicted number of aides that God has promised you to be there. Remember, Jethro told Moses that he did well in leading approximately 3.2 million people out of the Egyptian bondage but now it is time to minister unto them. He shared with Moses that he would surely waste away and the people would grow weary if he attempted to hear the individual needs of all of the people himself. Jethro conveyed to Moses that he needed assistants, qualified persons, to help ease the burden of the ministry. Moses was given advice to consult with the more important issues of the exodus while permitting those qualified and appointed leaders by him to address the other social as well as spiritual concerns. Blatantly put, it was going to take qualified help and Moses couldn't do it single-handedly.

The question that now needs to be addressed is, how large of a congregation are you serving or desiring to serve and how many assistants are there? I know that it sounds ridiculous, but it is an issue for us to review. Help me to understand the significance to a church of 600–800 with over fifty (50) ministers being licensed ministers, and what is the issue when the congregation is 400–500 and there are only two (2) ministers including the pastor? The actual number of assistants or associates will be predicated first on the presence of God and his will for the ministry and secondly the vision of the church and the submissiveness of the congregants to the move of God and their Pastor. The more

Commentary for the new Pastor

ministers that a church has don't always indicate a prosperous and thriving ministry *(ask Gideon)* and neither does having two or three ministers suggest a second-class ministry or third-ranked ministry *(Moses only initially had Aaron and Miriam)*. It is not quantity but quality. The most important issue is how well does the ministerial staff or teamwork together for the advancement of the kingdom of God.

> *For while one saith, I am of Paul; and another, I am of Apollos; are ye not carnal? Who then is Paul, and who is Apollos; but ministers by who me believed, even as the Lord gave to every man/ I have planted, Apollos watered; but God gave the increase. (1 Corinthians 3:4–6).*

Are they male or female Ministers?

Another concern for the called or new pastor and ministry is the gender of the Assistant, Associates, Elders or Lay Ministers, yes, their gender—their sex. Are they male or female? The topic of male or female ministers will vary from denomination to denomination; some denominations are more considerate than others or are extremely modest. Unfortunately and fortunately, there are still pastors who do not support nor welcome women into a called ministry position. A lot of Pastors would still desire to license an unqualified disabled man, rather than support a qualified able woman. For many ministries, the women are allowed to do Children's Ministry, Sunday school, or a comparative ministry, but, what about the preaching and teaching, the discipleship class and counseling, are they permitted to do that as well, *(my lips are sealed)*?

> Note: In my opinion, if there were more Women serving in ministry, counseling and worshipping alongside the Senior Pastor and his

Ministers, Evangelist, Missionaries, Associates, and Elders

vision maybe there would be fewer men in pastoral dejection and accusations.

The scriptures clearly state in Romans 16:1 that the Apostle Paul is charging the Church at Rome to receive a Woman in ministry as in the Lord and also to assist her in her ministry, *suggesting that she had the greater responsibility,* one of leadership and those assisting her were then under her delegation and authority.

Note: Romans 16:1–2, I commend unto you Phebe our sister, which is a servant of the church which is at Cenchre-a: That ye receive her in the Lord, as becometh saints, and that ye assist her in whatsoever business she hath need of you: for she hath been a succourer of many, and of myself also.

It is very imperative for us in this Ministerial generation not to miss our blessings and spiritual breakthrough because we have deemed it unbecoming to have a female ministering amidst our congregation. For those pastors or churches which continue to imply that females have no place in ministry or should only serve in a limited role, this should be respected as that person's or church's opinion and interpretation and should not be overlooked. One of the most rambunctious incidents you will ever unearth is a Pastor that supports female ministers and church members and leaders who do not or visa versa, so be prepared. *It is debatable.*

However, women are vastly hearing, acknowledging, and responding to the voice of God and are accepting their responsibility into the preaching and teaching ministry of the Gospel of Jesus Christ. Are they more than missionaries? After all, it

Commentary for the new Pastor

was a woman who ministered aside Moses, Miriam his sister, a woman who was the Judge of Israel, Deborah, women who told the Disciples that Christ had risen, Mary & Salome, and Women who ministered with the Apostle Paul, Phebe and Priscilla the wife of Aquila.

An additional aspect to consider, notice the women prophetesses, recorded within the Old and New Testament scriptures:

- Rachel (Genesis 30:24)
- Miriam (Exodus 15:20)
- Deborah (Judges 4:4)
- Huldah (2 Kings 22:14, 2 Chronicles 34:22)
- Noadiah (Nehemiah 6:14)
- Isaiah's Wife (Isaiah 8:3)
- Anna (Luke 1:36–38)
- Phillip's four Daughters (Acts 21:9)

If there are women who are sharing in ministry, *(who should also be qualified)* it is advisable for the Pastor and church leaders to pray for the ministry, pray that God will show the pastor and leadership what He desires to do through those vessels as they submit to your Pastoral leadership.

Training of Ministers—they are your Generals and Corporals

Most Pastors and ministries require that all Deacons and Deaconesses complete a predetermined trial period and then

Ministers, Evangelist, Missionaries, Associates, and Elders

graduate forward for ministerial authorization before an open or closed council session prior to being ordained. Now the question that I have is, if we require so much for the men and women who serve the people of God, distribute communion, and wear white suits on the first Sunday, how much more should be required for those who stand to preach that people will not go to hell and teach that others will not be tossed to and from by every wind of doctrine and counsel in faith that families stay together? The standard of training and equipping for Deacons and Deaconesses should not be greater than what is established for those who are "Ministers of the Gospel".

> *1 Timothy 3:6, Not a novice, lest being lifted up with pride he fall into the condemnation of the devil. (They cannot be licensed on Monday the first of the month and then become youth pastor or educational director the Monday of the second month).*
>
> *2 Timothy 4:5, But watch thou in all things, endure afflictions, do the work of an evangelist, make full proof of the ministry. (Every pastor must ensure that those who are serving with them in ministry have qualified their called, even if it means through a crisis or trials).*

Every minister, whether those who are fostered or adopted into your care or birthed from your ministry should be required to reacquaint his or herself with various doctrinal issues and continuing educational courses for their ministry. This education should include courses in Hermeneutics, Homiletics, the doctrine of God, the doctrine of Christ, the doctrine of the Holy Spirit, the doctrine of Salvation, the doctrine of the Devil and the doctrine of Eschatology to name a few. Every pastor should ensure that when training is secured for the ministerial team or staff, that it is:

Commentary for the new Pastor

a) to each pastors standard and requirement,

b) for the advancement of the ministry to where they are serving,

c) to assist the individual minister for personal growth,

d) to stir the gifts within the congregants,

e) addressing a variety of ministerial areas, for example counseling, leadership, etiquette and personal goals,

f) not in conflict with said churches doctrine and teaching, and

g) finally, not out of agreement with the Holy Bible

Unequivocally, the training and educating of the assistant and associate ministers should be a spiritual asset more so than a lateral impartation or burden for the Senior Pastor and Assistant. The education of the Assistants and Associates should be a willing experience and one that is challenging for those who embark upon this feat.

Working with ministers as a Senior Pastor can be a very good experience for all parties involved if each receives the other as being the God given more so than the enemy from within. Take time to get to know those who labor among you for no man can row a boat and raise the sail simultaneously; neither can a person be the captain and *shipman*, though the captain knows what the *shipman* is doing at all times.

CHAPTER FOUR

Church History

> And these words, which I command thee this day, shall be in thine heart: And thou shalt teach them diligently unto thy children, and shalt talk of them when thou sittest in thine house, and when thou walkest by the way, and when thou liest down, and when thou risest up. (Deuteronomy 6:6–7)

WHAT CAN YOU REMEMBER ABOUT YOUR PAST, SPIRITUALLY?

It is very pertinent for everyone to always remember his or her family and church history; knowing where we as a people, family, or society have originated from. People as a whole should know if they have migrated from Poland, Australia, Ghana, Philippines, Italy, or India for the walls of our past will eventually talk. The central purpose of church history is for us to see the events and progress in which God has permitted to occur within the genealogy of our lives and foreparent's journey

Commentary for the new Pastor

over the previous years, especially during the darken days when we thought that all hope had vanished.

(Yet history mostly conveys to us, *(who were not present)*, any and all transactions, distinctive occasions, and unique circumstances that have transpired prior to our arrival on earth or at this particular level of spirituality and place in ministry). Local church history again respectfully notifies and describes for us the life and events of those individuals and groups who have proceeded before us and their course of journey taken.

> *History provides those who make inquiry with the who's, the what's, the when's, the where's, and the why's, that which is welcomed and that which should be forgotten.*

Recant in your spirit Joshua 4:1–24, it was Joshua who told the people of Israel what God had said while they were crossing the Jordan River toward the land of promise. Joshua, under the obedience of Jehovah, gave and ordered twelve men, one from each tribe (Dan, Issachar, Zebulun, Reuben, Gad, Levi, Manasseh, Simeon, Judah, Naphtali, Asher, and Benjamin) while the waters were parted to pull a stone out of the Jordan River upon their entrance into the promise land. The stones would represent the twelve tribes of Israel and also serve as a memorial to God for him delivering them from the Egyptian Bondage. But more so as a chalkboard for a lesson of history, subsequently when their children and children's children asked what meanest these stones the Elders could give them a 400 year narration lesson concerning their past. Their chronicle was nothing to be ashamed of or forgotten, just something to catapult them into their destiny. I believe knowing the history of your ministry will also project you to where God has predestined you and your ministry to be.

Church History

Read excerpts for yourself

And it came to pass, when all the people were clean passed over Jordan, that the LORD spake unto Joshua, saying, Take you twelve men out of the people, out of every tribe a man, And command ye them, saying, Take you hence out of the midst of Jordan, out of the place where the priests' feet stood firm, twelve stones, and ye shall carry them over with you, and leave them in the lodging place, where ye shall lodge this night. (Joshua 4:1–3) That this may be a sign among you, that when your children ask their fathers in time to come, saying, What mean ye by theses stones? Then ye shall answer them, That the waters of Jordan were cut off before the ark of the covenant of the LORD; when it passed over Jordan, the waters of Jordan were cut off: and these stones shall be for a memorial unto the children of Israel forever. (Joshua 4:6–7)

Note: If there is no landmark of history, then the labors of others will only become as a rodent running through a repetitive maze—going nowhere, or as a dog chasing his tail—around in a circle scattering dust.

I have come to know that somewhere buried within the archives of every church assembly lays volumes of information that describes the mountains, the plains, the valleys, the good days and bad days that have ushered the local church to where she is now. If not written in documentary form then engraved on the hearts and minds of those who have walked in the moccasins of the Indian. Every Pastor should familiarize him or herself with this piece of commentary in order to know why various incidents are transpiring.

It is my opinion that the historical covenants of the church that each pastor should include and review should contain the following information:

Commentary for the new Pastor

- the year the church was organized,
- its time of incorporation,
- the council members and name of establishing churches,
- the location of the first church and the founding members,
- if there are any charter members,
- the founding Pastor, and the numbers of pastors who followed and their tenure,
- a copy of the articles of faith,
- a copy of the tax exemption filing, and
- all other applicable and legal documents.

Note: It is pertinent to know when the church was founded (even if it was first a mission) to accurately know from whence the church has come to promptly commemorate the anniversary of the church for spiritual and physical growth purposes from year to year.

The history record of the church should also mark the different locations that the body of believers has assembled, including the length of time that they may have worshipped in each building and the progress made while there. If by chance there were new constructions, improvements, demolitions etc. these also should be noted; but the most important recording of any church history should be the marking of souls, those who have been born again during the church's existence. So many times we mention the chicken dinners, the annual plays, the office purchases, the church picnics, the church anniversaries,

Church History

even the tea and fashion shows, but we never exalt the number of souls who have been converted. We forget those whose bowels have been refreshed and spirits rekindled because of the Word of God. If a church has not given birth to any new souls and have not born any fruit of her own, and yet have only recorded the names of church hoppers and runners—then the question should be asked, has there been any real progress? It is only a woman whose womb has been shut up by God that never bares children and it is the womb of the church that has been shut up by God if there are not any new converts.

> *Note: Every woman at some point becomes frustrated after continuously babysitting someone else's child and never giving birth to her own. Knowing that her nose will spread, her hips will broaden, and her ankles will swell is menial; she still wants to give birth to her own child.*

Who will gather the history

It is very important for someone qualified, involved in ministry and interested, to assist in keeping an accurate and dated history of the Church. The history of a church should never be tarnished, negated, nor forgotten even if there have been major struggles to keep the church into existence and even times pondered for shutting the doors. When considering the history, note that many negative issues as well as positive events may be revealed, including but not limited to why the Jones family hates the Brown family and why the Smith family assumes that they *run* and *own* the church. And if you ever want to be involved in a good fight try altering the church history without anyone's knowledge—you know, like removing someone's name from the roster.

Commentary for the new Pastor

One official church document!

Too often church members develop their own pages of church history, only documenting what they sense as being true, yet in reality it is often one-sided. There should be one official document for history with the church's seal and signature upon it for obvious reasons. Yet the most important reason is for legal purposes, for most lending institutions, corporate businesses, even city and governmental officials may need to know the time of existence of the church—especially if one is considering borrowing or obtaining financial support from a lending institution or receiving governmental grant money—especially now that there is more faith-based money available.

History is immensely important for us to understand because it lays a foundation to why people participate in the things that they do. As a new pastor or church leader the memoirs of the church will be important to you because it reveals the legacy of the church, the struggles faced, the spiritual battles incurred, and it also lays the foundation for which your trust and confidence will be built upon for the future of the Ministry. To not repeat the same mistakes as the previous administration or to reinvent the wheel, take the necessary time to review the history of which you have inherited. It really could orientate and boost your tenure.

CHAPTER FIVE

Prayer Service

Have respect therefore to the prayer of thy servant, and to his supplication, O LORD my God, to hearken unto the cry and the prayer, which thy servant prayeth before thee: (2 Chronicles 6:19)

PRAYER IS THE ESSENTIAL ELEMENT FOR EVERY CHRISTIAN AND CHURCH

While considering Pastoring a church, and becoming the spiritual leader, please note that it is vital and imperative to know the spiritual level of the church as a whole and not just individual members. As a matter of fact, you would be wise to know your own personal and spiritual level for praying also. If this can be accomplished you may be able to determine how strong the church's inner fellowship is, how spiritual the members are and how dependant upon God the church leaders actually are,

Commentary for the new Pastor

simply by attending the prayer meeting and service. Attending the service to see who is *(Tepilla, heb.)* calling upon the name of the Lord (Genesis 4:26).

Every Pastor needs to know the spiritual strength of the church he or she is making inquiry of. *Hello,* simply noticing who is there at prayer service and who is not there on a regular basis can determine a lot about the leadership and church's priority as a whole. Observing who is participating in the prayer service and then monitoring the prayer service can advise you if is it a traditional prayer service or if it is a real meeting hour to pray fervently for results. A man or woman of God who are lead by the Spirit of God can differentiate the difference between a typical prayer service and a meeting for prayer by who is there and what type of prayers are being prayed.

> *Beloved, believe not every spirit, but try the spirits whether they are of God: because many false prophets are gone out into the world. (1 John 4:1)*

> *Note: There should be others in attendance besides the little old lady with nothing to do; and there should be other types of prayers being offered before God inside the church besides, "Now I lay me down to sleep I pray the Lord my soul to keep, if I should die before I wake, I pray the Lord my soul to take."*

The prayer service

During the prayer service there should be what "Grandma" called old-fashioned snot dripping, tear dropping, slobber slinging and body jerking power prayers in each prayer meeting. The prayers of the saints of God should cause the hair to stand up on the inside of your ears which exalts the name of God, edifies the believers, and threatens the sinner to run from hell and repent

Prayer Service

from their evil ways. Somebody should recognize when the Church prays for the "Peter type" situations, that their "Rhoda response" will begin knocking on the door (Acts 12:1–18). You will read more later on this text in the following pages.

As "the new kid on the block," be advised to the following points when considering prayer meetings:

First, know when and where the church prayer services are held, there are some churches that do not hold regular prayer service (even at their own church) or the prayer service is not prayer service. But for some, it is a friendly gathering of church members to hear and pursue the latest gossip of the week and to signify regarding who shot John and if he died or not. It is true that some Prayer meetings are on Tuesday and Wednesday and some are incorporated on Friday's joy night service, however, it should not really matter as long as the saints of God are sincerely praying for a manifestation from God.

Let the record be stated, that there are no predetermined or mandatory days or date set as a rule for any church to have as prayer meeting time—for men ought to always pray and not faint (Luke 18:1)—Pray without ceasing. (1 Thessalonians 5:17)

The second point for consideration is, knowing who is responsible for conducting the worship service or meetings of prayer? Surely, there will be many who volunteer but the Senior Pastor is responsible for the spiritual oversight of every worship service. But who actually is responsible for leading the prayer meeting needs to be addressed and clarified—especially in the absence of the Pastor. Customarily, the Ministers and Deacons (if there are any qualified to lead) under the direction of the senior pastor or overseer have been appointed to conduct the initial

Commentary for the new Pastor

service of devotion and testimonial (modernly known now as worship and praise), and then progress into what the senior pastor has established.

The activities of worship can be from simple praise and worship to casting out of demonic spirits, to preaching and prophesying; depending on how *radical* of a worship service is welcomed by the ministry.

> Note: Prayer meetings are generally predicated on the atmosphere set by Holy Spirit, that particular ministry and the Senior Pastor. If you don't have a praying pulpit, there will be no praying pews. If you don't have a praying leadership, there will not be any spiritual disciples.

The third point for consideration is the time and length of prayer service or meeting. No said government, clique, social club, manual, nor individual has the authority to preestablish a set time for starting or ending the hour of prayer. However, it doesn't suggest either that in order to feel the power of God we need to be in a church building 24 hours, 7 days a week, 365 days a year for prayer, or position ourselves in a particular posture to be heard by God; but neither should we be more anxious to leave the hour of prayer than we were to come.

Every church will have members who choose not to posses nor demonstrate an eager spirit for prayer, (remember Peter, James and John were found sleeping, when they should have been praying with Christ) especially during the summer months. Summer months and prosperity have a tendency to make weekly activities become scarce of church members—that is until a crisis comes and then everybody wants to become a prayer warrior. This is what I call a situational prayer warrior. This situation determines when, where, and how long a person is to pray.

Prayer Service

Nevertheless, the power of prayer during the prayer service must be emphasized before and throughout the hour of prayer when the visitors and friends gather. People must know and recognize the need and influence of prayer that begins with an individual relationship with God. Be careful of people that imply that they have power, but are unable to demonstrate that same power in the time of a crisis. In Mark 11:22–24, the scriptures state that when we pray, we must pray believing that what we are praying for according to Gods divine will shall be done. If we are not going to exercise this privilege in prayer, then we must not even attend or host a weekly or monthly prayer meeting—*praying is not a joking matter.*

> *Note: Be aware that a regular meeting day and time for prayer will be essential to the spiritual success of your ministry. Prayer is the essential component to the church body as air is to our human body. No air, no life, No prayer, no life.*

Don't Gossip—Pray

Emphasis to the church body, there is no time allotted for church members to gather for the latest in Church news (also known as gossip), when there are souls of men and women which need to be saved and delivered, spirits of the downtrodden which need to be revived and refreshed, hearts of the infirmed that longs to be mended and fused, and minds of the distraught that necessitates to be clear and sober. Somebody needs to pray. Some parent or child(ren) needs to return home, there is a couples marriage that needs to be repaired, some church leader craves a place of employment, a family needs a location to call home or simply put to have the ability to think rational and sane; all this can be achieved when there are powerful prayer meetings. Now

Commentary for the new Pastor

to those of you who choose not to believe in the power of prayer re-read Acts 12:1–25, there the story is told in depth about Peter being put in prison, intending for his life to be taken after the Easter holiday to appease the audience of men. All of us have been in a situation familiar to this.

However verse 5b-7 says:

> but prayer was made without ceasing of the church unto God for him. And when Herod would have brought him forth, the same night Peter was sleeping between two soldiers, bound with two chains: and the keepers before the door kept the prison. And, behold, the angel of the Lord came upon him, and a light shined in the prison: and he smote Peter on the side and raised him up, saying, Arise up quickly. And his chains fell off from his hands (KJV).

> verse 5–7 TLB, But earnest prayer was going up to God from the church for his safety all the time he was in prison. The night before he was to be executed, he was asleep, double-chained between two soldiers with others standing guard before the prison gate, when suddenly there was a light in the cell and an angel of the Lord stood beside Peter! The angel slapped him on the side to awaken him and said, Quick! Get up! And the chains fell off his wrists!

Now on another note, if you don't believe that prayer is essential, Grandma also said just wait until the thunder cracks the lining within your ministry, or the lightening of despair zigzags across your vision, or drops of rebelliousness and contrariness reign, or rain of misery pours on what you thought was a sun shinning experience—even your sinful neighbors know that you will pray then. For prayer is, the cable that connects each saint of God, to his or her power source, in order for him or her to make it from one level of blessings to another. The only

Prayer Service

recommended way to receive the power needed is to enhance your time in Prayer with God.

A final point that Pastors typically are called to address for prayer service is, the code of dress for the duration of the worship service. The reality of the code of dress is typically aimed at women, for men can come in t-shirts, jeans, or even shorts. Yet, women have dress codes, which seems to be a double standard. Some churches disallow women to wear any form of slacks to church, for any worship services, even to worship with their heads physically uncovered. So the questions are; should there be allowed shorts in the church for men or women, how about spandex or jeans? Should there be men with earrings and children with cut offs?

Well, here goes an uncanny perspective, the most important concern during the midweek service whether noon or night, Tuesday or Thursday, is the sincerity and genuineness of that person's heart and spirit which no one knows as they are worshipping God and interceding on behalf of other family and friends—but God. *(1 Samuel 16:7c, for man looketh on the outward appearance, but the LORD looketh on the heart).*

Because God is looking at your heart don't become so traditional as the Pharisees, who were more concerned with the carnal, *(washing of brazen pots, inside and out)* that you miss the important part of ministry the spiritual *(ministering to the people of God).*

CHAPTER SIX

Finances

They gave money also unto the masons, and to the carpenters; and meat, and drink, and oil, unto them of Zidon, and to them of Tyre, to bring cedar trees from Lebanon to the sea of Joppa, according to the grant that they had of Cyrus king of Persia. (Ezra 3:7)

WHERE IS ALL OF THE CHURCH'S MONEY GOING?

A very vital yet complex and cautioned area for the new minister to address is that area of church finances—capital. *Taboo, Taboo, Taboo*—don't mess with the loot or mulah; Pastors are told. It is suggested to many newly elected pastors, *don't* ask about it, *don't* inquire concerning it, and *don't* worry in regards to it, just act as if there is none. Understand that from the beginning of a new pastorate, Ministers as a whole are generally labeled like a folder; they are labeled as a womanizer, a beer-keg sitter,

Commentary for the new Pastor

or money hungry from the beginning. Therefore, because of the pre-judgmental attitudes of people, the new leader must approach this area prayerfully, not in question or justification of his position and authority; but knowing that a soft answer turneth away strife (Proverbs 15:1).

Each Pastor should openly and directly without reservation to his ministry and for the future of his assignment needs to set in order the things that are wanting—with authority and confidence. No matter how much or how often the people *(those in leadership or the congregation)*, become disturbed made to feel uncomfortable or make lewd threats, it is the pastors responsibility to know where all finances are and how they are disbursed.

For if a Pastor is to lead and build a thriving, energetic, attractive ministry, structurally and spiritually then as they pastor, they must become a wise builder. A wise builder which sitteth down first to add up the cost before he builds that he will not leave off where he started. If a pastor is going to build a ministry, yes it is going to take finances; therefore, he must know the current expenditures and current income of the proposed ministry.

> *Note: Scripture affirms that it has always been the Priest, the Prophets, the Kings, and the Apostles that have managed the finances, or appointed the appropriate person to administrate over them, not the church Treasure, Deacon chairperson or the Secretary. (Acts 2, 5)*

It is the Pastor who will serve as moderator at the annual church business meeting or church conference and must give an accurate account of all finances received and disbursed by the finance and budget committee or the designated group. The Pastor must enlighten the congregation on where and how

Finances

the monies have been distributed and received, including from which accounts. If the pastor fails to act in this area of ministry, the people will make their own assumptions, which would be a great misfortune. So then, let each auxiliary and/or ministry in addition to the church treasure, comptroller, or financial secretary prepares the necessary reports for the pastor with precise accuracy. Know this, that being an Overseer, Pastor, Elder, Bishop, or Minister that the Holy Ghost hath appointed, will cause for you, the Pastor, to also oversee the church finances as well as the annual or monthly church fellowships with others and the church calendar. Let me forewarn you, to use additional caution while pastoring traditional churches which have set up rules and regulations that mandates every Pastor to spiritually address and obtain permission from the congregation or officers in order to fulfill their pastoral ob-ligations—*especially in the area of finances.*

> Note: Two curses that constantly emerge before the church are 1) tying or restricting the hands and vision of the pastor and 2) supporting the typical contribution of church dues before the tithe and giving as God has caused to prosper.

The church tithe and church dues

Each Pastor should know that leading congregations into giving of tithes *(ten percent of one's financial income)* when they have been accustomed to church dues, *(a set dollar amount, as in an secular organization)*, may take allowing them a grace period to become adjusted to your biblical and doctrinal position. Difficulties and challenging moments will arise, if they have not been taught or instructed correctly by the previous administration. Tension can also be felt if the previous administration hath

Commentary for the new Pastor

taken advantage of his or her authority while overseeing the church finances, the church may need more time in adjusting to your leadership before they will conform.

Things you must know about finances

First things first, every Pastor should know how many sets of financial books there are per financial account and institutions. Don't be surprised to discover that some churches operate out of two or three different sets of financial books and it is a guessing game to which is correct. It is not recommended to have two sets of financial records existing within the house of God, but we know that not all churches are honest churches and nether do they pretend to be. Keeping the financial books to a minimum keeps heartaches and problems to a minimum as well. This leads to the actual number of in-house banking and business accounts a church should have—one, this does not include certificates of deposits or mutual funds.

Depending upon the size of the congregation, how we number the parishners and the type of auxiliaries and ministries we have, will determine how many accounts that the church financial office should officially carry. Generically speaking, there is one checking account for the reception of regular tithes, offering, and church expenditures, one savings account or building fund account to permit the officers to invest wisely in the kingdom of God, whether local or abroad, one benevolent account used to distribute to the necessity of the saints in need. Any other financial account will be determined by any outreach ministries that may be under the direction of a nonprofit organization or Community Development Corporation within the church, i.e. scholarships, tutorial, childcare or feeding programs. If this is the case it is my opinion there should not be a separate financial

Finances

institution or bank account for each ministry, this can lead to problems—*NO, and this will lead you to problems unless it is strictly managed.*

Secondly, it is also important to know who is responsible for the church finances; is it the church treasure or is there a finance committee? It needs to be determined if the persons responsible are elected or appointed and if so, by whom. Also, depending on the size of the congregation, is there a comptroller, a financial secretary and or treasure— then knowing which has jurisdiction and final authority over the other? It is also important to know for what period of time they have been serving in these positions and the length of time they will serve in these positions in the future.

The wrong person in the right position can change the complexity of the entire church-negatively.

The possibility of one person being responsible for the accounting of the church for an extended period of time is very realistic, yet dangerous. I am not suggesting that wrongdoing has been done because of a person's longevity, just noting that the church's best interest should be at the heart of the ministry and not the desire to simply appease the current employee. In doing so, is also important to research what form of accounting system is being used and why (manual or computerized). What software will be used and if there is a church accountant, if so will an outside accountant or auditor in addition to the one serving in-house have access to the record books?

This is where we address the need of their qualification, for those serving must be qualified accordingly.

Commentary for the new Pastor

A need for a good financial team

The qualification of a good financial team is a must and one that can work with the vision (foresight and aspirations) of the Pastor and church may I add. Too often the qualifications for a financial team has been based upon persons book knowledge or their length of higher learning, training or education. In addition to these great qualities, there needs to be a spiritual standard met also. Know if the person(s) have a visible and active relationship with Christ and attends spiritual service involving the ministry where they serve. Is there a spiritual connection with the Pastor and ministerial team or just the love for counting money?

> For where the treasure is, there will also be the heart of man. (Matthew 6:21)

As a matter of fact lets get to the foundation of matters, *(take a deep breath and read slowly)* as pastor you will want to know: who writes the checks, who signs the checks, how many signatures are required on the checks, where are the financial books kept, who fills out the bank statements, how many bank statements are there, when are the weekly offerings counted, and by whom and when does it get deposited in the financial institution? *Breath again,* what if there is a weekly offering given, who sets the yearly budget, is there a limit on disbursements, is there a set amount on general spending or benevolent and mission expenses, is there a petty cash—if so, who is responsible for it and how much is kept in it? Is there an in house audit system and who makes the final outflow decision, are there any credit cards—if so how many, what are they used for and *(please find out who has them)*?

Please distinguish that every church is different according to the church policies and by-laws, *(review yours immediately)*

Finances

however there should be one governing principal regarding the Church's finances, which is the word of God. The word of God cries for the need of being a good steward, observe 1 Corinthians 4:1-2: *Let a man so account of us, as of the ministers of Christ, and stewards of the mysteries of God. Moreover it is required in stewards, that a man be found faithful.* For a steward is a person who has been entrusted with another person's treasure and or wealth. Those who are in finances are stewards entrusted with the wealth and treasure of the church members that have sown financially into the ministry and in response are expecting a harvest from good management.

Tithing envelopes must be used

Another item for consideration is for the Pastor to know the type of envelopes used and the markings on the outside. I admit it does sound trivial—but know your envelopes and what is mentioned on the flap or the front of the envelope—many envelopes have the persons name, address, phone number and envelope number and special fund markings listed with dollar amounts. All of this is done to help expedite the clerical process in recording the gift and to properly give credit to the contributing church member and or visitor, while making the dollar amount accurate for recording.

Many times marking the correct envelope with the correct markings can expedite the entire process. However, there are many envelopes that are generic in color and style and usually end up in the garbage can rather than in the financial office because of the inappropriate markings by the contributor whether member or visitor.

Commentary for the new Pastor

How much Debt is owed by the Church

Oops, I almost forgot a small nugget. While the pastor is observing the church's financial make up, it is also to their advantage to know the amount of financial debt the church has accrued over the past year or years. All debt is not bad debt or an unhealthy investment. Each Pastor must know the amount of debt owed out and to whom it is owed. To be perfectly forthright, there needs to be information ready and available, *provided by the treasure, finances team or comptroller* to describe the lenders name, address and phone number, account number, to list the debt status, the purpose of the debt, who were the authorized signors, the annual term with percentage rates, pay off amounts, and early penalties.

There should be a list provided to the pastor including but not limited to:

- church mortgage debt *(including annex),*
- property debt *(including onsite and offsite),*
- automobile loans, leases *(past and present),*
- the church parsonage mortgage *(including any rental property),*
- auxiliary financial obligations,
- copier and duplicator leases,
- computer and land line communication leases,
- mobile communications, and
- all credit cards, charge cards, and entertainment card statements and balances, these are also financial.

Finances

As the Senior Pastor you need to be acquainted with this information. Why? Because churches are taken legal action against for non-payment or slow-payment, and their possessions sold to liquidate the churches assets, churches have filed bankruptcy in the vein of similar institutions and finally receive credit reports on Brad-Dunn Street. Simply put, but yet so complex, a new pastor should know his or her ministry even regarding the area of church finances before the pulpit podium and office furniture are literally put on the curb.

CHAPTER SEVEN

Church Membership

But now hath God set the members every one of them in the body, as it hath pleased him. (1 Corinthians 12:18)

WHO IS A MEMBER AND WHO IS NOT, AND DOES ANY ONE CARE?

Over the past 25 to 30 years, it has become evident that the church membership role may be increasing, but the average Sunday morning service, as a whole is not showing the same pertinent growth. Many pastors are reporting 500 families on the church role but only 200 families in attendance and or 1200 families on the church role and only 700 families in attendance. Yes, I know that there are a few exceptions. It would be a fair assessment to state that once a minister enters the church he or she wants (or God commissioned him or her to Pastor), I am sure that he or she desires to make a difference (by adding to the numbers) in the local church, while keeping those members with

Commentary for the new Pastor

a little seniority present. However, before a minister involves him or herself with numbering the attendance on Sunday morning *(or even midweek)* it would be wise to concentrate and consider two primary points.

The first item each Pastor should consider regarding the church's roster is the number of members who are currently on the churches role; whether as an active member *(attends church regularly in an established time period)* or an inactive member *(doesn't attend church regularly within that same time period)*. It would clarify any and possibly all questions concerning the attendance on Sunday morning if you knew how many families and individuals have actually united, been baptized, and completed new members/discipleship classes as proposed by the church.

Analyzing the active and inactive membership of the church will involve detailed planning, observations and assistance from the Deacons ministry, faithful church members, as well as the churches secretary. An *active members* status should include those who participate regularly in Sunday morning service, prayer service, bible study, financial support, and any other stigma that the church has established as a rule without becoming to cultic in their practice. The *inactive members*, wow, *(everyone has them)*, don't be surprised that sometimes they out number the active membership of the church. However, they are members who join or unite one week and then show up sporadically as physical needs arise more so than spiritual needs, or when they feel compelled to do so—*(except in a crisis or church challenge)* then everyone desires to be a member.

Note: Christ would that we bare fruit and our fruit remain. (St. John 15:16)

Church Membership

Unfortunately, inactive members continuously feel as though they are an active church member, with all rights and privileges as others, because most inactive members do not know what constitutes them not being an active or inactive member—review your policy on this issue, it could be beneficial later on.

The numbering of the people is always a touchy issue, especially when you and I consider David and how he began to number the children of Israel when God told him just to go fight, when he was already winning the battles (2 Samuel 24:1-11). Underscore this thought—don't allow yourself to begin numbering the people *(especially when they belong to God)* for lucrative gain sake, or because you want everyone to be impressed by your attendance/numbers on Sunday.

> Note: Jesus said, I will add unto the Church daily, such as should be saved (Acts 2:47). Know who is doing the adding. Acts 2:41b, and the same day there were added unto them about three thousand souls.

If you have rationalized that numbering the people is an imperative or essential task, take it up to show accountability and commitment on your part, to those whom God hath appointed you over and not to compare to other ministries in existence. Make sure that your attitude and disposition is, that if one sheep leaves, becomes absent, turn out to be sometimee', you are prepared to take the necessary measures to leave the ninety and nine who have not left the fold to find the one sheep that is missing. The lost sheep is someone's relative, (Father, Mother, Son, Daughter) maybe yours.

Too frequently churches are only concerned with those who are there in attendance on Sunday morning, and not overly

Commentary for the new Pastor

troubled with who is missing. Because there will be people to join the church for various reasons:

- situational confessions,
- a crisis within their life or extended family life,
- a death,
- a loss of job,
- popularity of church, choir or pastor,
- convenience sake,
- Mother's Day, and
- Easter or Christmas.

Not all of the people who join the church will stay because of those same reasons. News flash, *"not everyone who joins the church will stay"* or should be allowed to stay.

I believe that is the dilemma we are confronted with anyway, we have too many people joining the church and not attaching him or herself to the vision of the pastor; nor allowing the church to occupy them. If there were more people being attached to the vision, there would be less people using the church as a revolving door. Once a person finally joins *"cliché'—join,* who really knows what type of a church member they will become, some may become an Ananias and Saphiara or Alexander and Demas. Who knows how active or inactive they will be anyway? Every church member should acknowledge his or her membership through their presence, their tithe or offering, their gifts unto the ministry, their time giving to an auxiliary or volunteering in some capacity. It is a blessing that people desires to join church, but remember this thought—if God permits you to have 5

Church Membership

members, 50 members 500 members or even 5,000 members are you prepared to minister to those that God has given to minister to their need as a total man? Many people talk about having a major congregation, a mega ministry but not all are prepared to counsel, advise, instruct, and share with them or minister to their needs. Are you prepared? If God gives you what you talk about having are you equipped to minister to them to impact and change their lives?

> Tell them to stop coming and joining the church and let the church get in them, so that they can attach theirself unto the vision of the Pastor and his or her ministry.

Knowing those that are connected to the family

Getting to know the members once they become a member is another hot item. Why does everyone think that the Pastor is to know all of the members first and last name on the spot, and their nickname? Why do the church members insinuate that the church is getting too big, impersonal etc.? News Flash—Heaven will have more people there than in your 500 member church, so what are you going to do then? Leave, go to Hell, and look for the rich man, it is crowed there too.

A final thought to consider for the sake of the membership is, to remember that the bus and van ministry of the church is a key to establishing and building a growing ministry. A thriving transportation ministry can affect your membership either positively or negatively. We will address the van ministry in another chapter. Yet, getting someone to drive the van or the bus on a regular basis can be a tedious task too—*I thought I would add that here as a bonus point.* Church members should be able to get in touch with the bus or van driver for transportation to worship.

CHAPTER EIGHT

Sick and Shut in

When Jesus heard that, he said, This sickness is not unto death, but for the glory of God, that the Son of God might be glorified thereby. (John 11:4)

WHO IS SICK, I DON'T KNOW, WHO IS SHUT IN, DON'T KNOW THAT EITHER?

*I*f there is one area that every Minister or leader should immediately concern himself with in the church that he or she is soon to be pastor of, it is the matter of those faithful members whose bodies have become weakened and/or where situations beyond their control has caused them not to be as visible as they once were, and now find themselves either home-bound or convolesant in a rehabilitation facility. THE SICK, THE SHUT IN, OR HOMEBOUND.

Ministers have been called to do just that—minister, to serve others, those who are in genuine need not greed. It is my

Commentary for the new Pastor

belief that ministering to a persons needs are more than simply distributing food baskets, attending court sessions and making their presence known at area police stations.

> *Then shall the King say unto them on his right hand, Come, ye blessed of my Father, inherit the kingdom prepared for you from the foundation of the world: For I was an hungred, and ye gave me meat: I was thirsty, and ye gave me drink: I was a stranger, and ye took me in: Naked, and ye clothed me: I was sick and ye visited me: I was in prison, and ye came unto me. When saw we thee a stranger, and took thee in? or naked, and clothed thee? Or when saw we thee sick, or in prison, and came unto thee? And the King shall answer and say unto them, Verily I say unto you, Inasmuch as ye have done it unto one of the least of theses my brethren, ye have done it unto me. (Matthew 25:34–40)*

> *The Spirit of the Lord GOD is upon me; because the LORD hath anointed me to preach good tidings unto the meek he hath sent me to bind up the broken hearted, to proclaim liberty to the captives, and the opening of the prison them that are bound. (Isaiah 61:1)*

Therefore, as you come into a new church for ministry, understand that the ministry is not simply confined within the sanctuary walls on Sunday mornings, preaching a favorite sermon for the fifth time, or twirling around in your office chair, but effective ministry extends to those who are elderly, to those confined to a mental or penal institution, sick, or shut in *(young and old)* to bring about a productive change in their lives. Real ministry in my assessment extends beyond the church's physical grounds and into the communities where the members reside. Ministry begins on their turf.

Sick and Shut in

A caring shepherd for hurting sheep

A compassionate shepherd knows when one ewe lamb is hurting and proceeds to mend the wounds back together. If the pastor, *regardless to the size of the congregation,* cannot visit or oversee the visitation of the church body where he or she serves, it is his and her responsibility to ensure that the hospitalization team, ministers, elders, deacons, or deaconess share in this responsibility *regularly, and not seasonally* and if not, then real ministry is not being performed as Christ desires. It should not even be so much of a concern to the type of sickness, the length of illness, or the cause of the failed health of the member; the concern is determining whom, if not the Pastor, is responsible for the visitation.

If there is one area or quality that church members are inclined to see in their Pastor, other than good preaching, teaching, singing, and being dressed in a nice attire, it is a heart that demonstrates care, love and compassion for every member and not simply showing favoritism as a Pharisee of old—*especially toward those in Gay clothing.* Gay clothing is, the attire that is of the latest fashions and design, typically worn by those who are of the upper echelon class. In today's society it would be those from the corporate world to those on Wall Street or another part of the influential world. It would include those who are society's big marble shooters to those impressive long-time church members. Anyone with clout could fit that mold.

Who visits the sick and shut-in

Jesus himself stated that, those who are well need no physician but those who are sick, ill, weak, and suffering from infirmities need a physician to address their condition. To suffer from an infirmity is not confined or limited to those who have just

Commentary for the new Pastor

experienced some surgical procedure, an automobile accident or even birth defect. Being sick and shut-in also identifies those who have been afflicted mentally, emotionally, psychologically, or even socially. Question, so who visits them? Answer:

- those who are first qualified,
- secondly, those who sense this as their specific area of ministry,
- thirdly, those whom have been commission and or charged by the pastor,
- fourthly, those with an compassionate heart to serve, and
- finally those who have been invited by the ailing member or family member to do so

Visiting the sick and shut-in, can also be the responsibility that is delegated to a certain group of individuals, i.e. the mission, men's ministry or women's ministry. Typically it is an assignment especially for the deacons, deaconesses, and elders of the church (*specifically those who are assistant ministers on the rostrum, who traditionally awaits an opportunity to preach in the pulpit*). These individuals in addition to those who are seasoned mothers of the church and missionaries' can and should be responsible for visiting those who are convolesant as well as serving their needs, including communion and minor house cleaning.

Note: Ministering to those who are convolesant includes those who are at their residence or a relative's residence, a nursing home facility, or another form of care center—even prison.

Sick and Shut in

Consider this, he or she may be in deficient, poor, or inadequate health, *but all sickness is not unto death* which typically is no fault of his or her own therefore this does not suggest that they should be overlooked and treated as an insignificant inatomate item who cannot perform up to their previous ability. Hear me loud and clear; there are some church members that have been and are able and will continue to assist the ministry though they are physically confined at home or to a nursing home. As a matter of fact, from there many members will fervently pray for the church, *and God will hear them there*, the Pastor and their ministry as well, and without reservation send their tithe to continue the financial support for building of the kingdom of God.

Our strong recommendation is to visit the sick and shut-in, even if you have to devise a temporary schedule that outlines calendar rotations of people who need to be ministered unto and who is responsible for ministering unto them. The schedule can be weekly or monthly, or as necessary for ministry.

Matthew 25:36b, I was sick, and ye visited me:

Special note: In my opinion, it would be catastrophic to learn that the person who was sick, shut-in, or convalesant is now demised and you now have the exclusive responsibility to attempt to eulogize one of the church members who you never visited or known while they were under a Physicians' care. I understand that it is not possible to know all 5,000 members by name, but cell groups will sure make a lot of sense.

CHAPTER NINE

Visitors

And some days after Paul said unto Barnabas, Let us go again and visit our brethren in every city where we have preached the word of the Lord, and see how they do. (Acts 15:36)

GUESS WHO IS COMING TO YOUR CHURCH

If the Pastor and church desires to win people to Christ, experience lives changed, have souls saved and increase the physical membership number of the church there are going to have to be visitors. *Yes, those who are not regular members.* We generally classify visitors as—those whom are not *"official"* members or those who may not have officially united with that particular local assembly and have attended the new members classes. They may have experienced the worship service on many occasions but they are still "visiting." They may already be Christians and members of the Universal body of Christ but

Commentary for the new Pastor

they have not publicly acknowledged their desire to be members of that particular *local* assembly.

Let it be known, visitors also known as guests come to church for various reasons. Some visitors are curious to the grapevine happenings, some are invited guests of a current church member, some are vocational transfers from another town or state searching for a new church home there will even be disgruntled church members from another church visiting your ministry looking for a simple breath of fresh air.

> Fact—some visitors are basically unsure of why they are visiting where you serve, but now that they are, don't miss an opportunity to minister to them and their family.

Therefore, it is the responsibility of the Senior Pastor, the Ministers, church officers, and worship leaders foremost to be concerned for the visitor's presence. Including those visitors who are:

- Politicians,
- Substance Abusers,
- Recovery Addicts,
- Vacationers,
- Situational Attendees, And
- Those Periodically Looking For a blessing.

Take notice, to some visitors are those who have come to church for the very first time perhaps, well, actually the second through the fourth time, that may be a member of another church,

Visitors

or maybe not. Yet they have not united with that particular assembly where they have been frequenting.

The question now is not who visits but what do you do with the visitors once they arrive and/or leave? How can you decipher between first time visitors and the regular church members? What happens to the one, 10, 20, or even 30 people who come to your church, fill out a visitor card and then deposit them in the offering tray or specified receptacles week after week; some you meet others you don't—but what happens to them? Did they even receive a visitor's card, a phone call from the ministry, a letter or postcard in the mail, or even a personal visit from the ministry team—which? We invite them to come and they show up but what do we do with them afterwards? Too often churches are guilty for being negligent about visitors.

With visitors, there should be some form of follow-up done even though you may not be able to reach every one of them for membership or they may not all come back. Ask yourself some basic questions, how are the visitors treated once they arrive? Are they shown where the lavatory facilities are located, how to get to children's ministry, why Deacon "Smith" sings five hymns, what to do during the offering period, or communion fellowship? Are they told how to schedule a meeting with the Pastor or other ministers and counselors? Are they given instructions on how to receive audio and videotapes? What about those who need transportation—are they informed? Church *hospitality* should begin from the moment the visitor arrives in the parking lot; hospitality begins with the members who walk in with them, to the usher or greeter standing at the vestibule or sanctuary door.

Commentary for the new Pastor

Emergency note: (Members should not treat visitors—let alone other members—as if they have the hee'-bee' gee'-bee's or the whoo'-gee'-ha'gees). We all can use a little help there.

Another question that every pastor will have to address at during another period of time is, what have each visitor taken home with him or her after the worship service, besides the sermon—if they take that? Every church should ensure that there is some form of literature available that describes the pastors and church vision, giving a general oversight of each church ministry, which also welcomes them, even inviting them to set an appointment with the pastoral staff. They should have access to a complete listing of phone numbers to be able to contact a church officer or leader regarding the activities of the church.

> *Note: If you don't have qualified persons with the ministry to serve the visitors as they fellowship with you during your services, don't just confirm any Tom, Dick, Harry or Robert within their presence; not all church members represent the ministry as you would have them to towards non-members. As a matter of fact this will be the reason that many people will not return to your ministry. You may think that it is because they did not enjoy the preaching or choral singing, but all the time is was because of the irate church members acting indignant—yes, even as a Christian.*

Once there is a system in place, as approved by the pastor, whether it is a book to sign members in or cards deposited in a general receptacles. Geographically each ministry should know where the visitors migrate from where they are going, but most importantly, what are you doing with them while they are there with you besides praying for them and inviting them back to another service?

Visitors

I applaud every ministry that is meeting the total needs of their ministry, especially reaching out to those who are non-members, providing them an opportunity to fellowship with other members of the body of Christ. Remember we are all one body in the Lord Jesus Christ—even the visitors.

CHAPTER TEN

Keys

And the keys of the house of David will I lay upon his shoulder; so he shall open, and none shall shut; and he shall shut, and none shall open. (Isaiah 22:22)

HE WHO HAS THE CHURCH KEYS IS IN CONTROL

The church keys, AHHHHHHHHHHH—who has them and why? How many sets are there?

This has always been a dilemma within the local church regardless of the denomination and the physical location. Everyone *(well not everyone literally)* has a tendency to want a copy of the front door key and even distribute a copy to his or her nephew or niece. People love to have keys, whether or not they know what they are for; why—*keys are a symbol of power and authority.* This is easily seen when Christ told Peter he had

Commentary for the new Pastor

given him the Keys to the Kingdom and he must exercise them with caution, (Matthew 16:19). He was given authority.

There are some church leaders that have copies of church keys, and yet they don't utilize them appropriately or with the authority that has been given unto them, especially as it relates to ministry opportunities. If someone has a key, it should be because they are using it for ministry related purposes and not simply to impress his or her peers and coworkers. Nothing is more dangerous and nerve wracking than to have church members with keys and not knowing what they lock and unlock.

It is not unheard of that whenever there is new leadership, that there are also new keys, new tumblers or new locks etc. but remember *this is costly*. However, some locks on the contrary have not been changed in five or ten years and thusly creating an opportunity for every Tom, Dick, Harry and Robert to have a copy. Listen, if a church officer has a set of church keys, they should not make a copy and give to Sister Pricilla in order for her to gain entrance to the church for mission meeting because she gets there an hour before it is time. It is advisable to the Pastor, church administrator, or trustee not to become so liberal in distributing keys just so that a particular choir, ministry, or auxiliary can have access when they choose, there needs to be some regulation.

Example: If there are 20 auxiliaries and each auxiliary has a key because they want to be able to come to church and fellowship or hold meetings when they get ready, then there are 20 keys out and therefore 20 additional opportunities to have errors and the door left unlocked. Left unlocked so that the Sunday school tape player can easily walk out—*the devil is a lie*. Listen, she may be the church mother or church historian but she doesn't need a key. He may have lain the first brick, signed his name on the credit

Keys

application, but he doesn't need a key. EVERYBODY DOES NOT NEED UNSUPERVISED ACCESS TO THE CHURCH.

Note: Too many keys out, lessens the security of the church and the property that is insured, which the members have invested their gifts and talents, lock it up.

Because of the lack of and inappropriate security measures with most churches there has been an increased need of some form of an alarm system to be installed. There was a time when you could leave the church unlocked all week long, let alone have an alarm system, and things would be as it was left—but times have changed in our churches, just like within our neighborhoods. Yes, times have changed. Times have changed where you need to know who has keys to the church and to what purpose are they being used. As well as for and the extent of the security system, whether bells, whistles, and/or bars.

Whew, and that only describes the keys to get inside of the church.

Now that you are in the church, investigate, discover, do what you can to find out who has keys to the secretaries office, the Pastor's study, the deacons room, the choir and/ or musician room, the audio/video room, janitorial room, boiler room, baptistery room, supply room, kitchen, kitchen cabinets, kitchen pantry, computer/lab office, elevator mechanical room, the bookstore, filing cabinets, board rooms, or the outside shed. Not to mention, who have the keys to the church vans, bus, tractor, file cabinets and safe deposit boxes.

Commentary for the new Pastor

Keys are major symbols of authority; and people love to jingle the keys, but all should make sure that the right person has the right keys. If you don't know where the keys go or to what they are used for—then as Pastor your responsibility is to investigate it. It is a possibility that many people have made the church out to be a shoplifting, five-finger, and sticky hand place to assemble, to pick out their next marketing product for the neighborhood rummage sale.

Who is designated to lock and unlock the Church

Typically it is the church trustees that have been designated the responsibility of the church keys and security. They have been charged with unlocking and locking up the facilities and grounds of the church. It is policy in many churches for most trustees not to have key copies to everything but they should have access via a location designated for all keys to be stored *(which is a locked and secured place)* that will allow them access. The location of the general church keys should be in an agreeable place for other designated person to have access to for church related instances that needs immediate attention. If it is not the church trustees that have this access then it is the maintenance or janitorial team that maintain the keys.

The maintenance or janitorial team should have keys that will provide entrance to:

- the main doors,
- supply rooms,
- janitorial rooms,
- elevators and service areas,

Keys

- all rooms and entrances that are required to be maintained, and
- any area that may have chemicals stored, any storage sheds or emergency entrances or exits.

But the most important concern should be for the Pastor to know who is in custody of the church keys and for what.

When in doubt to whom has keys and who does not, consider changing the tumblers and gain control of this area, it may cost more than what you desire to financially invest or cause the budget to be greater than what has been established. However when it is established, then designate a responsible person to then oversee this area of ministry. This is an important area of ministry as well.

CHAPTER ELEVEN

Parking Lots

And he delivered them into the hand of servants, every drove by themselves; and said unto his servants, Pass over before me, and put a space betwixt drove and drove. (Genesis 32:16)

BUT IF THEY ALL COME, WHERE WILL THEY ALL PARK

It may appear to be a small endeavor, but knowing the size of each parking space, the general location, the number of designated handicap spaces, as well as any courtesy parking spots (*i.e. for pastor, pastor's wife, musicians, deacon and trustee chair*) is something that should always be addressed and taken into consideration for each church parking lot regardless to the size and number. Having insufficient parking or inconvenienced parking can and will affect the attendance of your worship service on Sunday's and during weekly worship service—for people generally don't like to walk a great distance, especially if

Commentary for the new Pastor

they are coming to church. The only time that Church members normally like to walk or will walk is while they are going to the mall to participate in a sale during Easter, Thanksgiving or after Christmas sale.

When making an allowance for adequate parking to accommodate the current and prospective church membership and visitors, it is vitally important to account first for a proper location. Location, Location, Location is everything. Yes, I understand that parking is generally on the site where the church is located; however there are many instances of a need for overflow parking or future parking. Future parking is something that is not normally considered until it is to late, once the new church has been erected or the current church is packed to the walls and then there is a city code violation.

Parking in the correct spaces

The average number of parking spaces required by most zoning department is one (1) parking spot per four (4) people occupying either the sanctuary or fellowship hall, which ever is greater. If there is not immediate parking space that is owned by the church, then offsite parking should be considered; especially if the parking spaces considered are within 500 feet of the sanctuary. *(People are going to learn to walk for the Kingdom).*

Until then, your neighbor next door, the school parking lot, adjacent daycare facilities, shopping plaza, strip mall, or even the doctor's offices traditionally will negotiate with you concerning your usage of their facility, especially if and when you are not using your lot to the fullest capacity they can share with you. It will be advantageous to peruse these areas of negotiation, especially if you are land locked by their presence or someone else on either side.

Parking Lots

Most city codes also requires that there be a minimum number amount of handicap parking spaces which are clearly marked near the main entrance and exit of the church building, where the handicap accessible ramp is located. If this is not currently implemented or active, then each ministry should consider appropriating funds at some point in the very near future to accommodate those in need. It will also be accommodating to those who are elderly, who continue to find the ministry advantageous and attractive. Remember, no one except those who have been issued an authorized and valid handicapped sign are permitted to park in the handicap area and if a member or visitor is found to be illegally parked they can be fined up to $200.00 by the local law enforcement agency.

> *Remember, you need to know how many parking spaces you have, and then know how many spaces are designated for office staff, handicap and any other special allocation, however this often subtracts from the general parking facility.*

Lighting and security of the parking lot

Unfortunately every ministry is not fortunate to be located in a well to do neighborhood. Many who believe in and practice a grass roots ministry will find themselves surrounded by a neighborhood of people who have a tendency to visit the church parking lot while their owners are in worship. Therefore, most ministries, especially those who are midsize to large, have security parking or parking lot attendants to puruse the lot during the worship service. This is done for several reasons, one to provide extra security for those who would be potential victims of neighborhood thieves and vandals. Secondly, for those who would ask (yes) folk steal on Sunday, and any other day of the

Commentary for the new Pastor

week from the Church parking lot (*not to mention from God in the offering receptacle*).

Often times, there are individual(s) who serve, as attendants or security guards and they are either church volunteers, paid staff workers, or outside security workers. Please note that all have their own disadvantages as well as advantages, yet each ministry has to utilize what is beneficial for them. Some points to consider when employing parking lot attendants and security guards are, how often will the worker serve the ministry, will it be daily, weekly, monthly or even bi-monthly, will they be hired workers, will they carry firearms and if so, are they licensed, bonded, and insured? It is also beneficial for each Church and Pastor to implement an emergency plan as preventive measure in case of an altercation within the parking lot area.

You will also need to consider, are the workers adults or even college students, what will their responsibilities be, valet parking, the general circling of the parking lot, and what are the wages if any? As a matter of fact, since they forfeited the worship service will a video or audio copy of the message be made available to them or is there another way for them to receive the message?

One final point to consider is, if the parking lot of the church is leased or owned by an outside group, organization or company. It sounds ludicrous for something of this nature to actually take place; until you live somewhere like San Francisco or New York where land is as frequent as snow in Africa. So this forces some churches to lease or enter into some form of financial agreement with the property manager of a grocery store, strip mall, restaurant or school. Know where your parking lot(s) are and know how well lighted or unlighted they are. Yes, lighting is a concern also for church members, especially after bible studies, choir rehearsals

Parking Lots

and evening services. It is to my belief that those who attend the Worship services in the evening have a right to safety and security, especially within their own church parking lot.

CHAPTER TWELVE

Church Supplies

And David prepared iron in abundance for the nails for the doors of the gates, and for the joinings; and brass in abundance without weight; Also cedar trees in abundance: for the Zidonians and they of Tyre brought much cedar wood to David. So David prepared abundantly before his death. (1 Chronicles 22:3,4,5d)

WHO PURCHASES WHAT, AND WHERE IS IT KEPT?

Church supplies seem like a menial item for the success of a growing ministry that is until you run out or something doesn't get delivered on time. The purchasing, storing and distribution of church supplies is always a tedious task. It becomes a monotonous assignment to know about the supplies, because no one really wants to do this job, especially the Trustees. Yes, I said Trustees for my experience has been that some feel their

Commentary for the new Pastor

only assignment is counting church finances on Sunday. The trustees have assumed that it is the maintenance department or janitorial departments responsibility—some suggest that it is also the office staff responsibility depending upon the supplies. It is true that there has to be a separation between Church supplies, (toilet tissues, paper plates, salt, groceries etc.) and Church Office supplies (copy paper, pens, pencils etc.) It is suggested that four venues be considered when determining how to set-up and utilize a working system to manage each.

First, who does the purchasing and reordering of all of the church material? Who is the Joseph type that knows when to buy and sell corn as if on Americas' Wall Street, in order to reduce cost and increase profit? It is vitally important to know the person or persons who have been appointed to make purchases for the church in each category respectfully. Too often there is a lack of supplies in various areas because no one was told to order any supplies or no one was informed of what was needed. There only needs to be one person primarily responsible for ordering and purchasing the necessary supplies for the church with a backup person in case of his or her absence. When this is the case, they must follow the pre-established format and attempt to establish their own.

There should only be one person to minimize any confusion or excessive products on hand, which drives up the budget for that particular department. So when this person is ordering, he or she will take various things into account i.e. are there any promotions incentives, what are the most frequent commodity used, are there any special requirements during holiday season, funerals, or conferences? What is actually needed and when? The person responsible for the ordering should know the rotation of the stock, not to keep too much or too little on hand.

Church Supplies

Secondly, from which account are the items being expended from? When purchasing is done, each area (of supplies) should have been assigned a certain budget amount for the year. This dollar amount will take into consideration any special and upcoming events. Upon each receiving a budget amount to work within, it should also be specified to which account the funds will come from so that there is no confusion about what account is to be taxed.

> Example: if the church clerks needs pens and pencils, will this come from the supply or maintenance account, the church general account or because it is a low ticket item—from the on hand petty cash?

As a matter of fact it should also be predetermined if they are or are not permitted to borrow or purchase for one another. Many times if one person is out they have a tendency to call back and ask if the other needs something and they will purchase it for them out of their auxiliary account. This is very risky and also affects the budget amount set at the beginning of the year. Each should have their own account to work out of as the financial secretary or comptroller has designated for proper accounting principals.

Third, Where are the items stored and who has access to them? Wow what a wasted question—not so. Especially if there is a large order placed and there is nowhere for it to be stored upon its' arrival. If the person responsible sees a once in a lifetime sale for some non-perishable items and orders them, what and where shall they go once they get there—who shall deal with them? One of the biggest problems churches have is storage, because most only have a vision for the sanctuary or office space and not where

Commentary for the new Pastor

the tools, (toiletry items, copier paper, ice salt, or envelopes) are going to be stored.

In conjunction with this, it also should be stated who has access to the toilet paper, paper towels, pens and pencils. Some members feel that since they tithe, or give generously from time to time, they have an right to these items if they are running low at home, no they don't—tell them I said so, that it is stealing from the house of God. Access to these supplies should be limited and not easily accessible, especially from people who are not responsible for these areas. Access to the supplies should be off limit, especially for maintaining order in the stock and budget areas. Everyone should not be permitted in some areas of the church regardless to if they have or have not been a regular tither or giver.

Finally, it must also be known where all of the supplies are purchased. Yeah I know this should be a no-brainer or an item that needs not a lot of attention but—it does. Many times discount stores and wholesale business are the key to obtaining the product needed while other times they are not going to meet the need. Every custodian, janitor, or sanitation engineer, secretary, or who ever should know the difference between a time to save money and the time to purchase good quality products. Some areas within the ministry don't require name brand products while others are a must. However, checking the label for ingredients and manufactures can reveal more than what the eyes and nose can detect.

- Items that should be brand name: Certain cleaning supplies, eatable and perishable items, material that are made accessible and marketable to or for the public.

Church Supplies

- Items that can be generic: Partial cleaning supplies, throw away items, tissues and paper supplies.

Therefore knowing where to shop is very essential for cleaning products, office furniture and supplies, and outdoor equipment, also knowing who is responsible for the same is just as important.

If we can take it further, there may be a person within the church that has a professional cleaning company, office Supply Company, or a distribution site for goods to be sold in bulk as well as by the unit. Purchasing from a church member, whether it is through Amway or some other bulk center, can work for the church ministry or against the churches vision. Every ministry has to explore their own opportunities for efficiency and know with whom they are doing business and if it going to be profitable for the ministry as a whole. Every opportunity that looks and sounds good may not be advantages to the church as it is being marketed.

CHAPTER THIRTEEN

Church Store Accounts

And over these three presidents; of whom Daniel was first: that the princes might give accounts unto them, and the king should have no damage. (Daniel 6:2)

YOU CANNOT DO BUSINESS WITH EVERYONE, OR EVERYWHERE

*E*very church has store accounts, either at Sam's Club, Wal-Mart, a Christian Bookstore, Office Max or somewhere comparable. What is most important is not where the church accounts are, but to know who has the ability to make purchases in the name of the church and for what dollar amount where the accounts are located. Oftentimes, the church purchaser has been a person who has not been qualified in this area to do so, but because they have demonstrated an attitude of willingness, a spirit of availability, and have been in the church for an extended period of time they automatically become the churches purchaser. Also

Commentary for the new Pastor

because of these generic qualifications they in essence hold possession of the credit cards and have access to writing and signing church checks to acquire requested or desired merchandise.

Every pastor upon their arrival should inquire concerning the church's accounts and then know who is authorized to write the checks for repayment, for this is as critical as who made the purchases. Unfortunately, everyone may not want to hear nor accept the fact that they are not qualified nor designated to make certain purchases in the name of the church, though they may have a willing spirit to do so. Only those who are properly authorized should shop with the church's account number, and the churches money at DIY, Sam's Club, Home Depot, or Super K Mart etc.

> Note: Everyone who writes checks for the church and signs the checks should not have the freedom to do the purchasing as well. This would be the fox watching the hen house mentality.

It can become vary irritating when the wrong people volunteer to do what is someone else's rightful responsibility. Praise God for a willing spirit, but there needs to be better control of the churches accounts and those authorized to act on behalf of the ministry. For whenever a church account is set up, this also gives access to the person opening the account or making the purchase the right to use other information that is normally kept confidential.

> Example: they come into contact with the church tax identification number, churches financial history, churches past and current credit ratings, all of which should not be to everyone's accessibility.

Church Store Accounts

All church accounts need to be properly set up and established for convenience sake of the ministry and business and not according to one-person specification or liking—especially since they have attended some workshop or conference. All accounts should list on file who is authorized to purchase: gas, books, spoons, towels, light bulbs, pencils, pens etc. and for what dollar amounts. Then there also needs to be an in house audit or check system to ensure the same, making sure that the receipts match up with the check as well as the bank statements issued. This ensures that "past" Superintendents of school, current deacons, or youth leaders do not try to purchase any books or material for him or herself after their term is expired. It does happen.

Note: Let me be the first to tell you, that the Saints have taken advantage of lucrative gain opportunities at the expense of the church for their own personal benefit.

When deciphering who has what authority *(let alone who issued it)* on which account, it also needs to be specified what the terms are for repaying the account. Various companies offer different repayment terms therefore, it should be noted if it is: net 10, net 30 or even a net 90 day term, indicating when payments are due to bring the account balance to zero. This will avoid any late penalty fees as well as finance charges that could be incurred.

Minimizing or maximizing your accounts

It is also recommended that each church keep to a minimum the number of accounts that they have open, as well as the credit cards distributed to those in leadership. Simply because the business offers you an account doesn't indicate that you should

Commentary for the new Pastor

accept or open that account. Operating from too many accounts can be as detrimental as utilizing too few accounts. As a matter of fact it is not the number of accounts that matters, as it is being mindful of the individual who is in charge of what transpires with each account. First note, each store account that the church has accumulated and engaged to do business with should be a legitimate account and reputable business. It would be to the church's advantage to always deal with trustworthy companies and not someone recommended by a church member to stop by and pop-open their trunk for the latest in software, Tupperware, cleaning supplies, and Kleenex.

The person responsible for the church accounts should also review the monthly statements for billing errors, overbilling or even double billing; if this is not the responsibility of another person and/or department of the church. I know someone may not think that billing errors are possible on behalf of the said business, but it happens everyday even to or with *"Mega Church"* ministries. Because it happens every day, there is a strong possibility of funds being mismanaged and unaccounted for or items listed that the church did not authorize or purchase. Businesses, banks and church officers make mistakes, just as we the consumers make them and therefore the church finances team, budget team, accounts receivable department, or designated person should keep an open observation for said concerns. It should always be the church purchaser, church treasure, comptroller, or financial team that consistently and regularly review statements from the store as well as from the financial institution for accuracy.

It is also my opinion that all church accounts whether retail or wholesale, distributors of produce or electronics, should also be treated in a professional manner at all times. Every opportunity from the representatives of the church should do all to avoid any and all possibilities of souring the relationship or bringing a reproach unto the church's name.

Make sure the right person makes the right purchases for the right results

To ensure accuracy in church purchases:

- a "check and balance" system should be initiated within the ministry that gives a listing of items purchased, items used and where, and a count of all items remaining,
- proper documentation should have been completed by the store manager or authorized persons, with the signatures of the authorized church representatives and a copy kept on file,
- the church should have a certain dollar amount on what each individual is allowed to charge or purchase before an additional signature is need or additional authorization is needed,
- more than one person should have access to and a working knowledge of what is being purchased from which store and by which authorized church member, and
- there also should be an "up to date" rotation of products within the ministry.

When church accounts are established, this is when and where having the knowledge to manage a church as if it were a *"for-profit"* entity is advantageous. The church finances must always operate in the black and not in the red. Only those who are authorized must utilize their God given abilities to make sound

Commentary for the new Pastor

decisions that are in the best interest of the church and not their own. Remember they are all representing the Kingdom of God.

CHAPTER FOURTEEN

Church Mail, Mail Boxes and Email

The cloke that I left at Troas with Carpus, when thou comest, bring with thee, and the books, but especially the parchments. (2 Timothy 4:13)

FROM SNAIL MAIL TO INSTANT MAIL, YOU GOT E-MAIL

One of the most overlooked pieces of administration, but yet one of the most significant, is the church mailbox or the Post Office box. I know pastor you may not believe so, but answer these questions quickly in the next 30 seconds: who is responsible for retrieving the mail, where is the mail receptacle located, is there a post office box (if so who has the access and the keys), who is responsible for distributing the church mail and office mail, are there in-ner-office mailboxes, does the church have email, who is responsible for retrieving the email, who has access

Commentary for the new Pastor

to the mail account, have you ever missed your mail or received it well past the post marked date? Well, is it important?

Note: The churches mail and mailboxes are generally overlooked because it is automatically assumed that the church secretary receives the mail and then distributes it to the appropriate departments and personnel.

Not all of the time will the church secretary gather the mail. Other office secretaries or clerks may be designated to retrieve the mail from the mailbox or even the main post office to prepare for interoffice distribution. As a matter of fact it is true, some churches also have *"witty trustees"* and *"members"* who believe that it is their responsibility to trace, track, screen and monitor the mail since it bears the churches name on the envelope. Without hesitation this behavior should be deemed unbecoming as a leader and member of the congregation where you will serve.

Note: If you pray for God to send you a check in the mail, how would you know if it came or not, if you don't know who is retrieving the mail and if you don't know if this is a team or ministry that can be trusted?

Proper reception and distribution of the church mail is significant for the success of every ministry. Consider the Bible, and the sixty-six inerrant books that Jehovah God instructed his scribes to pen, and then his mail carriers to deliver. Consider the writings of Moses, as he recorded the books of the Law, the Major Prophets and Minor Prophets as they penned the books barring their name. Also take note to the Apostle Paul and how twenty-one letters are accredited to him for writing. Now

Church Mail, Mail Boxes and Email

answer this question, what if the mail (letters), which God has intended for us to receive, somehow was fumbled in the delivery and never was received by us—the recipient? Better yet, answer this question, what if the mail (letters) that was intended for the Israelites regarding Jehovah being their God and they being his people was delivered to the Canaanites or the Jebusittes—that would have been a major catastrophe. The same would have been a misfortune if the letters that the Apostle Paul had written to the Church at Philippi, blessing them had turned up in the mailbox of the Church of Laodicia. It may be extreme comparisons for some to digest, but there is still a reality of the importance of distributing the mail in the local Church where it is addressed.

To avoid mail discreprecies, it is important to establish two basic guidelines for all office personnel who are receiving and distributing the mail.

1) There needs to be an established time for picking up the mail, either onsite or from the central or main post office and,
2) to continue the keeping of peace about the mail, it should be determined who is going to retrieve the mail and then ensure that it reaches the correct person(s), especially mail that is time sensitive or marked personal and confidential, and marked for the pastor.

It is strongly recommended that the person who is to distribute the mail, be trained with regards to what to look for in identifying where and to whom the mail is intended for. Some correspondence marked foreign missions may not need to go to the Senior Pastor but to the mission ministry or the evangelistic

Commentary for the new Pastor

ministry. The utilities of the church, or any "bill" i.e. telephone, gas, water, electric, mortgage, or even copies of leases should always be forwarded to the individual who is responsible for writing the checks or for warded to the person designated by the senior pastor. Regardless to whom is designated and who is not, no mail should be hanging out of the persons back pocket or within the purse of the individual who collected the daily mail.

Those who sort the church mail should also be highly trained to transact business with confidentiality. Some Pastors have designated the Secretary to open all mail in order to properly determine where and to what department should receive it and some have not. If by chance a member or even a nonmember writes into the church sharing confidential information for the counselor or pastor, the person receiving the mail should not read the entire mail as if it was directed for them. *They should be advised to practice discretion.*

Getting the mail where it belongs

It should immediately be established by the pastor what mail is to be opened and what mail is to be opened only by the addressee. Yes, some pastors prefer their mail opened and highlighted for the mail subject, while others request that their mail be sealed and only opened by them—*this is what I prefer and practice.* Handling mail is a very important responsibility because of the information sent as official or original documents, the content of the material, the sensitivity of time, and nature, and the final destination for the mail to reach.

Some churches have progressed from placing mail on a table to actual operating mailrooms, where mail is sent out from and received into. Mailrooms today *(in the church)* are similar to those socially employed, but they have ministry as its main

Church Mail, Mail Boxes and Email

focus. Many mailrooms not only deliver mail but also receive and distribute orders for the ministries audio and/or cassette ministry. Now if this is the case, then the mailroom functions as a small distribution center and not the typical mail service. So, as a person volunteers, or as they are elected to service the incoming and outgoing mail ministry must be part of their character.

Email, dot org, dot net, dot com, everyone has it

Now, because of our modern day technology we also receive electronic mail via our computers, also known as email. Almost every church, Pastor, office staff has email and the churches email should not be confused nor melted into the office staff personal email. Every staff worker may or may not have an email address but surely most churches have one generic mailbox where all mail is received whether it is for the Pastor or office staff. If so, this should be handled with professionalism and confidentiality at all time.

Many Pastors as well as staff workers may have their own private email address, which is not related to church ministry. Regardless if this is the case or not, if email comes to the church address, then the church secretary should review it carefully, knowing whom the sender is or if it is private then the pastor should receive it for confidentiality purposes, unless a specific person has been given clearance to make the appropriate decision in addressing it.

When reviewing email, exercise caution, especially when viewing attachments. Viruses, junk mail, and electronic information that are not ministry related are infecting many computers. If you happen to permit the office staff and personnel to open mail and use the churches email address, be careful that it is not abused for their own personal gain and also advise them,

Commentary for the new Pastor

as pastor you have the right to view anything that comes across on the churches email system. Mail is very important regardless to the method. It serves as the link of communication from one person to another and one place of business to another for a healthy and productive relationship. A lack of communication is only fuel for confusion.

CHAPTER FIFTEEN

Offsite Church Property

Now Joshua was old and stricken in years; and the LORD said unto him, Thou art old and stricken in years, and there remaineth yet very much land to be possessed. (Joshua 13:1)

THE PROPERTY THAT YOU SEE, WELL, THERE MAY BE MORE

There have been many discussions held in regards to the church owning property. The question has also been asked if the church should own property or sell property for profit. It needs to be understood that over the course of time, the church will become the owner of more property than where the sanctuary is located. Historically this has been acquired through seller and buyer transactions, but also through the church being named the beneficiary in someone's estate or will.

Commentary for the new Pastor

Other questions have been pondered by many church members such as, how much acreage should the church own, where should the church land assets be located, is the purchase price the right price or is it simply what the church must do? Others have also inquired if the church has acquired enough property for future building projects. All of these are good question to ask, but it is going to take a spiritual ministry team to answer and address many of these questions as they work with the vision of the pastor. If there is not a spiritual ministry team embracing the vision of the pastor then the church will not even own a one-room building for worship.

One of the most disheartening issues facing a pastor is having a ministry team, an executive board of directors, or an administrative director which does not have an in depth vision for ministry to see the need or purpose to acquire additional property for the future expansion of the church.

> Note: Speaking by permission and through experience, I believe that the church should acquire all the land and other profitable property around their sanctuary as possible (through purchasing or donation acquisition).

By purchasing additional land adjacent to the current sanctuary, this will keep the church from becoming landlocked by other potential buyers and later having to purchase the same property for more than its original or previous value. As a matter of fact, the question has been opposed, if the church should own property away from its current location and if so how much and what purpose will it serves in ministry? In today's society, it is very feasible and viable for churches to own and gainfully employ other property such as, Housing developments, Beauty and Barber

Offsite Church Property

salons, bookstores, restaurants, clothing stores, and carwashes to name a few. Since our government has engaged many faith-based initiatives, there are many churches gaining in real estate as well as other significant humanitarian and philanthropic opportunities, which is advantageous in more ways than one. It is to a church's benefit to own more property *(land and building)* than the lot that they worship on, who knows when a large company or benefactor will donate or purchase property from or for the ministry.

Note: If a church owns these types of businesses, they are also creating opportunities for their own qualified church members to become gainfully employed and/or to receive the necessary training they need in order to seek other job prospects.

Psalms 24:1 states, that the Earth is the LORDS' the fullness thereof, the world and they that dwell there in. Since this is what God hath revealed to us about us and for us as his children, why should the heathen prosper more than his children in Finances, Assets, Investments, Business opportunities, Properties, or Land? God hath purpose and designed for us to own and to have possession of land and material wealth and therefore we should move to occupy what God hath predestinated for us to own, even if our enemies currently inhabit it. Listen, if God hath destined us to dwell in the land of the Canaanites or the Hittites, that only indicates that God is going to move the enemy out of the land, clean the land up so that we can occupy the land promised, even if we have to wait, but God will do it. Our dilemma as a people is that we want to go straight from bondage into the Promised Land, without being hungry, thirsty, cold, and troubled. When in fact God desires to kill everything within our lives twenty years old

Commentary for the new Pastor

and upward prior to possession. There are many people festering twenty-year-old issues; carrying old baggage with them as they move toward our promised land.

Things to question regarding the property

Therefore, when a church owns property there are certain stigmas and concerns that cannot be avoided by the most astute person or business minded couples. So when a piece of land or property is acquired or liquidated by and for the church, the pastor or administrator should always raise certain questions.

Example:

- is the proper afore mentioned clear of title,
- are there any current liens by private or public holders,
- what is the geographical location of the property,
- what is the current tax value of the building and or land,
- when was the last official appraisal and for what dollar amount,
- is the land adequate for current and/or future ministry,
- have there been any recent appraisals done or land comparisons (*if so make sure they are within city and county limits of said property*), and
- have there been any site and/or soil borings or any environmental testing done, bluntly stated is the property worth the investment or would it be an extra (*more than what the church currently needs*) burden for the ministry?

Offsite Church Property

If the land or site is being considered for business usage, retail clothing, an accounting firm, a credit union or such, the question that needs to be proposed is, has it been determined what the potential annual income for each proposed business will be in conjunction with what the expenditures that are projected to keep the said location energetic and fruitful? Every wise man must sit down and compare the pros and cons though he is a man or woman of God walking by faith—we should use everyday intelligence as well.

Basically and bluntly put, is the property a worthwhile investment?

When there are multiple pieces of off site properties, another necessary issue to make your priority is answering an additional set of inquiries. The first is who will manage the properties? Who will care for the property, the painting, lawn cutting, the repairs, the general upkeep, home inspections, and who pays the taxes etc?

Two sources for property management are 1) qualified church officers, and 2) an offsite property management firm. Yes, there are pros and cons to each however; individual churches and their leadership must determine what is in their ministries best interest. To be very candid, it is disgraceful for the church to own property and businesses in the name of the church and in representation of God, *(who owns everything)*, yet they never continue the necessary maintenance in order for it to be profitable to own by the ministry. If we as a people maintain our residential property with flowers, plush carpet, and Ivory tile should not Gods' property be professionally maintained as well?

Commentary for the new Pastor

What is wrong with this comparison?

Your home	God's house
• Plush carpet	wood floors and carpet remnants
• Gold chandlers	refurbished florescent lights
• Side by side refrigerator	your old broken handle, hand-medown refrigerator
• Complete A1 sound with a 15" horns	a sound system from the pawn shop
• Kentucky blue grass lawn	gravel spread over where the grass should be

One last thought to digest when speaking of church property, it is imperative for us to know if the property is under the name of the church or has it been titled to a subsidiary of the ministry or even an individual name. It should be common knowledge for us to ask, does "Kingdom Ministry" or "Joshua's Pentecostal Assembly" own the property? They both are connected together, but yet functioning with separate 501©3 tax exemption numbers? One is for the benefit of the Church and the other is the pastor's personal ministry. Therefore, it needs to be determined if they are operating with separate board members or are they both governed by and under the same authority?

When owning property, there should be a business plan that graphs the current budget and prospective budget, a business budget, and a spiritual vision for the property that wins the unsaved to Christ, basically a plan that will become beneficial

Offsite Church Property

for the total man and the entire ministry where you will serve. Remember you have been charged to occupy and possess, now go forth and build the kingdom of God.

CHAPTER SIXTEEN

Deacons And Trustees

But if I tarry long, that thou mayest know how thou oughtest to behave thyself in the house of God, which is the church of the living God, the pillar and ground of the truth. (1 Timothy 3:15)

THE CHURCHES GOVERNING BODY, SOME SAY NOT

The office of Deacon and the position of Trustee are the two most debated and misunderstood offices within the local church. Great controversy has aroused the spiritual nature of the church because of the discussion regarding deacons and trustees. What are they and who are they? What are and are not their social and biblical responsibilities? These are some of the concerns that church members will have. It is true that there are different denominational interpretations, but there is only one biblical interpretation.

Commentary for the new Pastor

Let us first briefly define the word Deacon, which is *diakonos* or servant not *doulous* or a bond slave. It should be duly noted that Deacons are servants to the Pastor and unto the church as the Pastor has so designated them—*(read Acts Chapter 6, since most people use this as the inception of the Deacons, and 1 Timothy chapter 3 for their responsibilities)*. There you will discover the Apostles appointing the holy men of God to serve as assistance to the people of God and not asking for anyone to volunteer. Contrary to what has been assumed historically, Deacons are not supervisors, snoopervisors, authoritarians, dictators or delegators. Deacons are servants, *ser-vants, ser-vants,*—they *serve* where appointed. They assist in Ministry for the furtherance of that particular church's ministry, to build the Kingdom of God.

The Chairman and Co-chairman are both important positions of leadership as they are the spokesmen for the entire ministry team. They are not more or less important than those who serve with them. As a matter of fact, if a man does not have the ability to be the Chairman of Deacons at any given time, maybe they should not be a Deacon at all. Therefore, it is the Pastor who will determine the length of service for the Chairman and Co-chairman of Deacons and the other Deacons who serve with him; I am sure you heard otherwise. For the office of Deacon or once a Deacon has been appointed and ordained as per the requirements of that local church, the bible, and Pastor the same then determines their tenure and authority.

One thought to consider is, within many churches once a man is ordained as a Deacon he is a Deacon for life (based upon his credentials and passing the criteria set), though he may not be appointed to the Deacon board or serve on the board annually at that particular church. Generally speaking they are for life, with

Deacons And Trustees

the piece of paper (ordination certificate) in their hand. When a man is considered for the Deaconship, surely they are observed for a specific period of time proving they are worthy of being a deacon. For in 1 Timothy 5:22, we are commanded, to lay hands suddenly upon no man. Yet it is the Pastor's right to ordain a man or keep him on trial (the time in which he is being observed) for observation for a longer period of time if it is deemed to be necessary (1 Timothy 3:10).

> Note: Beware Pastor of Deacon transfers. Those that come from another ministry and announce that they are a deacon; know that every person who proclaims that they are an ordained deacon, might not be—Pastor, require that they show evidence and credentials.

You will discover that many churches have at least two or three Deacons per 30–40 members; there is really no set number. So if a church has 800 active members, then most churches will have approximately 20–25 active Deacons, if you don't, don't worry and panic and don't run to volunteer Fred or Michael just to have some body—*it is going to be alright*. Choosing a body just to have somebody will be more stressful than blissful. However, the number of deacons, the length of tenure, the meeting day and times are all pertinent issues to be negotiated for the benefit of the majority of Deacons and the Senior Pastor.

A new pastor and a traditional Deacon Board

Each Pastor who begins their recent pastorate at a new place of ministry should use caution in going into a new Church where a pre-existing Deacon Board is responsible solely for the care of the church. Depending on the period of vacancy of a Pastor,

Commentary for the new Pastor

one (Deacon board/ministry) may have assumed the position of pastor (in authority only—not title). Meaning the Deacons may have gained position to have everything and everyone answer to them and once a pastor arrives they may continue to jockey for the same authority. Because of this, conflict can arise between Pastor and Deacon. *(Lets pray now for those who are there ... ... Amen)*.

> *Did you know that the word, phrase or term board is never use in the Bible when referencing ministry but it is only mentioned when the ship that the Apostle Paul was sailing Capsized? See: Acts 27:39–44*

Better yet, the conflict that often occurs or exists in church is between the Deacon ministry and the Trustee ministry *(who, possibly were already in conflict before the issue of a new Pastor arose)* on who has what authority and whose responsibility it is to do such and such and who really does it. Biblically, Deacons are within their given right to hold an office but the position of Church Trustees are not known to be a biblical office, though their actions are visible and their responsibilities are represented in the bible respectfully.

Know this, trustees have been established and put in place, first at the recommendation of the Secretary of State, in order to hold in trust all legal documents of the ministry (real and fixed, building, land and equipment) and should need arise, be able to liquidate all assets within the churches jurisdiction to fulfill any and or all unmet obligations *(Biblically the Apostles held the Finances, until the Holy Men of God (deacons) were appointed by them to perform this task—Acts chapter 6)*. This is why the church was bringing their personal finances and resources unto the Apostle Peter in Acts chapter 5 and Ananias and Saphhira (husband and wife) were cursed for lying unto the Holy Ghost.

The word Trustee is not found in the Bible

The Trustee office is not seen as a biblical office as the office of Bishop or Deacon is according to 1 Timothy Chapter 3, but their responsibilities of holding in trust, security, and stewardship the property of another is throughout the entire bible, and they should be found faithful in all things (1 Corinthians 4:1). Yet, there is enough evidence in scripture to support the position of trustee in the Old Testament and the New Testament. Joseph was trustee of the possessions of Pharaoh (Genesis 41:37–57) and the Ethiopian Eunuch was trustee of Candace the Queen possessions (Acts 8:26–27). The bible even makes mention of the unjust stewards and trustees (Luke 16:13). The Trustee's most important responsibility is to be faithful in regards to the church's property and to care for the said property as the owner would and occupy until he comes for accountability, not taking the resources and burying it for safekeeping's.

Let me interject this thought—though a trustee does not have to be a member of the church in order to sit on the "*Board of Trustees*", and the word Trustee is not mentioned in the bible, as far as the Secretary of State is concerned it is anti-Church, anti-Scriptural, and anti-Biblical to employ someone to oversee the spiritual finances, property and legal documents of the church if they are not a Christian and a regular church member. Might I add, one that demonstrates good spiritual financial principals as well.

Commentary for the new Pastor

Trustees must be spiritual

The same type of spiritual qualification that is in place for a Deacon should also be mandated for the Trustee or Steward. Within the local Church, each trustee must be more spiritual in heart than book smart in the brain, it has been a problem with most churches that receive people as members of the trustee board or ministry that have math degrees, economic degrees, and political science degrees but not a clue regarding biblical principals of financing. They might be experts at investing into mutual funds, stocks, money markets, and bonds but know that biblical principals are slightly different within the church than in white collar America. In the church, there has to be more faith than sight. If the trustees appointed do not have more faith in God than in his or her own ability—they should not be there—I repeat, they should not be there. It is a major position of authority to be in as a trustee and it is going to take a strong believe in Jehovah God for answers. A strong faith will be required regardless to the type of trustee said church endorses: there are four different types of trustees.

Types of Trustees

- General Trustees - oversee the general, legal, financial, and business transactions of the church. They hold all titles, deeds, etc. in trust while overseeing the maintenance and purchasing as well.

- Working Trustees - Specifically oversee the maintenance and property of the church; actually participate in the labor process.

- Business Trustees - Specifically oversee the business, planning, financial budgeting, legal affairs, check signing,

bank loan negotiations and any liquidations or purchasing in the name of the church.
- Deacon/Trustees - They are ordained Deacons, who serve as spiritual assistants to the Pastor and congregation and double as the legal administrators of the Church.

From counting and banking the finances on Sunday, if there is no finance team, to cutting the grass Monday-Friday, if there is no landscaping company, to the general maintenance and repair of the church all the way down to the purchasing and selling of property is the responsibility of each trustee ministry. For the upkeep of a ministry for the kingdom of God is a major part of a growing ministry. Each pastor must review terms and policies as it relates to the church trustee extended authority and who reports to whom. NO Pastor should want to be where they are constantly challenged, despised, and scrutinized let alone having his or her hands tied by a tight fist Trustee.

CHAPTER SEVENTEEN

Secretaries

Then Jeremiah called Baruch the son Neriah: and Baruch wrote from the mouth of Jeremiah all the words of the LORD, which he had spoken unto him, upon a roll of a book. ...Therefore go thou, and read in the roll, which thou has written from my mouth, the words of the LORD in the ears of the people in the LORD'S house upon the fasting day: and also thou shalt read them in the ears of all Judah that come out of their cities. (Jeremiah 36:4, 6)

DOES YOUR SECRETARY REPRESENT THE MINISTRY, OR IS IT JUST A JOB FOR THEM

Do you know who makes the first impression of your church, has it been discussed; surprisingly it is the secretaries and receptionist. Most people in the church and even those who are not in the church believe that the pastor is the person who makes the greatest impression upon the ministry.

Commentary for the new Pastor

Allow me to pause and interject a significant statement for consideration: *the secretary and receptionist makes one of the greatest impression of the ministry for those who come into contact with the church on church grounds; but every church member makes the most lasting impression with those who they come into contact with outside of the church grounds.*

Yet, it should be common knowledge that every person who contacts the ministry will be affected by the receptionist, church secretary and/or Pastors secretary/administrative assistant, and should therefore conduct him or herself accordingly. Therefore, it is the senior Pastors responsibility to make sure that there are qualified, pleasant, tolerant, outgoing people representing the ministry in these positions. The Church and pastoral secretaries can either help or hurt a growing ministry simply by what is said and done to those who contact the ministry. Within their responsibilities, they have the greatest consistent communication with the church community and outside community than most people posses within the ministry.

Secretaries are more than typists; they are the liaisons between the pastor and church and the professional, corporate, general and church world. Many times when the Pastor, lay Ministers, and officers are unavailable the secretary will be the person to assist the members as well as non-members until the correct person becomes available.

> *Note: It is going to take more than a person's willingness and talent to serve as secretary, it is going to take someone who a) demonstrates the fruits of the spirit, b) knows and supports the pastors vision for the ministry and able to perform it, c) have the ability to discern between members business professionals who are in seriously need or just desiring extra personal attention, and d)*

Secretaries

finally someone who can perform the task assigned to him or her with minimal supervision.

There are three important factors that each secretary should consider while serving in ministry—as a matter of fact, each pastor should ensure that these three areas are addressed as well prior to accepting and filling the position.

What about Character

The first area of concern should be observing the secretaries character for ministry and not simply job skills. There is an immeasurable difference in being a corporate secretary for IBM, Goodyear, and AT&T then serving inside of the house of God. Some people believe that you can conduct yourself as well and wear the same type of attire in the house of God, as one would while working in corporate America. Not so. Just because a person has the ability, skill, and knowledge to type 85 words per minute without error and keep coffee on the table for the staff doesn't indicate that they have what it takes to represent the Kingdom of God through a local assembly. Neither does it say they have the ability to represent you.

There are issues within the ministry that will be dealt with, seen, and experienced that will require a spirit of confidentiality and professional character that are different than in a business community. Therefore, a secretary's and or administrative assistant character would need to be operating at a high ministry level. Each person who shares as the church secretary or the secretary to the pastor must realize this is a position of ministry not simply opportunity and if the character of the secretary doesn't reflect the ministry, then that secretary doesn't need to be as visible as they are, even if it warrants termination.

Commentary for the new Pastor

The second area that should be of a concern regarding the secretaries or administrative assistants', is their ability to work with minimum supervision in corresponding by letter or phone as designated by the Pastor and ministry. Every office staff personnel should know that there will be a lot of time sensitive material that will be distributed via letters and phone, no pastor should have to lean over the church or pastor's secretary's shoulder to screen or monitor their behavior regarding their performance. That's where knowing the pastor and vision of the church connects with the position that the secretary is serving. Minimum direction should be given to the Secretary to conduct the necessary transactions for the advancement of the Kingdom of God.

Due to important information and many astute and professional personnel having an ongoing relationship with your church and ministry, the secretary (who represents you) has to be able to correspond in a timely and professional manner with each realizing that everyone deserves to be treated with respect and confidentiality and your ministry needs to be presented as a qualified ministry and not as some back yard "*hoopla.*"

Church communication is very important, whether it is via letter, facsimile, email, or another form of telecommunication and those who serve should be more than a person who only desires to work 4–6 hours a day, with only plans to leave out of the house to break the monotony of life. Oh, I must add, each Pastor should also be careful in hiring their relatives—I had to say that there. Because some pastors determine that it is the right decision to make for their wives, daughters, or sisters who need to get out of the house—my advice, pastor exercise wisdom in this area.

Secretaries

The third area of concern that pastors should be concerned with while considering a secretary is their ability to greet visitors, take messages, schedule meetings, and keep accurate appointments for the pastor or other areas of ministry as assigned. In other words, those person's organizational and personal administrative skills are important; as equal to their character being acceptable to the ministry. If the person you are considering to employ is unorganized and a walking basket case, then he or she will bring that same system into the ministry where you are asking them to serve the church and pastor.

Listen, some issues regarding the ministry are taught other circumstances unquestionably will transpire naturally, and then there are some administrative assignments that a number of employees will just not be able to perform. Know this, business is business and friendship must be separated from the ministry; and if a person doesn't have the ability to perform then they just don't have it. God has gifted us all in multiple areas and church administration may not be a *"wanna be"* secretary's gift. Take to heart, when a *"wanna be"* secretary does not have the gift of administration, the ability to keep things organized, and the wherewithal to systematically, chronologically, and structurally perform a specific obligation; many churches and pastors will miss important engagements, events and appointments and if they have not missed them they have been tardy.

If the Pastor has hired a church secretary and/or someone to assist him or her and the ministry, then the church and the pastor should have the right to communicate with those whom he has business with in a professional and timely manner and the secretaries have the responsibility to ensure the same without any excuses.

Commentary for the new Pastor

Compensation for the Secretary

Now another issue to be concerned with is compensation for the secretaries. We will address more on compensation later, however when considering compensating the Secretary three things are very important.

The first thing that should be considered is if the position of Secretary will be part-time or full-time position. Many church secretaries are part-time, depending upon the size of the ministry; and therefore part-time secretaries should not expect to be compensated as a full-time secretary. Neither are we suggesting that they be treated in a menial fashion either. Compensation for the Pastor's secretary or Administrative Assistant, may be slightly different than the church secretary's simply because of qualifications and work load however, having a vast difference in pay can create a war between offices because secretaries talk—smile.

The second point of consideration for secretary's compensation is the experience of the person(s) that are being considered to be hired. Many people who think that being a church secretary or pastors secretary doesn't have a specific criteria is WRONG. There needs to be an criteria set and established for meeting the expectations of the ministry. Too often we allow the standards of the church and ministry to be compromised in order to accommodate an unqualified staff member, including the secretary because we don't want to offend their feelings or because they have been a church or family member for an extended period of time.

> *Note: confidentiality, tact, professionalism, discreetness, code of Christian conduct will go a lot farther and be more appreciative than typing 70 wpm or getting coffee. Secretaries should be experienced with this type lifestyle because it should be a daily*

Secretaries

practice for them; anyone per se' can file, get donuts, unlock the office and copy hand—outs, but everyone cannot demonstrate the genuine character of a Saved Secretary.

The final note when considering a secretary is if the position is permanent or temporary for them. Often times it is said, "until you get something better you can always work at the church". Listen, it cannot get any better than working at the church. Never allow or permit someone to consider the secretarial position of the church second or third class rate, it doesn't even flow in that vein. It needs to be clearly stated when you are looking for a secretary that this is a position that should be respected and if no one from within the church/ministry is qualified to fill this vacancy you should not have reservations contacting a Temporary agency or listing the opportunity in the local newspaper for advertisement. The position of secretary is not some trivial place of ministry but one that comes with the possibilities of blessing or cursing a ministry. Therefore don't be afraid to examine three, four, or five applicants in order to have the right person for the right reason in ministry.

Qualifications for Secretaries

To do the job of a secretary means to do the job right. How can the task be performed and accomplished to the correct specifications if the secretary who is serving does not have the skills, talent, or desire to complete the necessary assignments in a professional manner? Every secretary and/or administrative assistant should possess a minimal amount of education and training that will enhance their ability to achieve as well as represent the ministry in which they serve.

Commentary for the new Pastor

As a pastor, one of the most disenchanting occurrences that have transpired amongst our ministry because of a lack of qualification has been letters delivered from the office with spelling errors, spreadsheets, and reports that are inaccurately compiled, conference paraphernalia mistakenly typed, and then some. This is primarily because the secretary does not posses the basic skills to know the difference between a red pen and a blue pen. Secretaries must be skilled enough, professionally adequate, but must of all spiritually sufficient to write, present, and distribute the correct literature or letters of correspondence to the correct office as designated.

Yes, a secretary should be required to attend workshops, conferences, seminars, or even classes at a particular University or College in order to provide them with the precise tools to accomplish the assignment given. Therefore, it is also my opinion, to ensure that each secretary have been given a) an appropriate job description, b) an opportunity to improve their skills, c) yearly funding to support their conference attendance and d) samples of the type of letters that are to be sent out on behalf of the ministry.

Some of the basic qualifications for the potential secretary should be a working knowledge in the areas of: shorthand writing and dictations. Even knowledgeable with software programs such as, Microsoft products, Spreadsheets, Financial program, English composition, and some form of design and graphic program. This will assuredly be to their advantage.

If you have any reservation about a secretary don't hire him or her. It is always easier to reconsider someone than it is to dismiss someone who has a desire to serve but is unqualified.

CHAPTER EIGHTEEN

Van Ministry

And he made him to ride in the second chariot which he had; (Genesis 41:43)

HOW ARE WE ALL GOING TO GET THERE?

Church transportation has always been a major issue that will need to be managed. Major in the voice of knowing who is going to provide the transportation and who doesn't think that it is really necessary. There are always lengthy discussions referencing transportation, especially from those who are actually in need. Being transported to and from church is no longer as it was in the days of old; for then everyone assisted in helping church members as well as visitors get to and from church. People were transported *via* neighbors' horses and buggy, mules, wagons, even given piggyback rides. When they were able to purchase an automobile—a

Commentary for the new Pastor

car, they made as many trips necessary to accommodate those who inclined to attend the worship service.

Let the record be noted, that times certainly have changed, everyone is pushing other visitors and members off on any one but themselves, including the church van or bus. I believe if God has blessed you with transportation you should minister to others in assisting them with transportation to and from the church. Yet, everyone now appears to rely upon the church van. The church van is now responsible for transporting the members to and from Sunday church, to and from bible studies, to and from prayer service, to and from youth outing, to and from Sunday school, to and from dinners, to and from shopping venues, and even to and from business meetings—everywhere that permission is granted, people suggest that the church van should take them.

Understand, that if a ministry has been blessed with one van or twenty vans, I believe that there should be transportation provided, to minister to those who are legitimately without transportation and who are commonly in need. However, there are some concerns and observations that each pastor should have clarity on as he or she indulges him or herself into this area of ministry.

Qualifications for driving the Van

First, it is my assumption that every church has someone who will and has volunteered to drive the church van. This is not a major concern, yet, it is always favorable when people volunteer their time and effort in this area however, as pastor it is your responsibility to ensure that each driver is qualified to drive the church vehicle. The qualification to drive the church vehicle is different from driving your own personal vehicle—because now

Van Ministry

the church becomes liable for any and all matters involving the vehicle while in motion in the name or purpose of the church. Therefore, each person should be examined for a valid drivers license, if the vehicle carries more than sixteen passengers they should posses a current Commercial Drivers License (CDL), if there are any moving violations on said license, and if they have taken enough concern to acquire the minimal liability insurance for their own vehicle and self.

The second concern for the van ministry *(since we are talking insurance)* is for the office personnel to know who is covered under the church's insurance or umbrella and if this is a greater expense because of the driver(s) previous history. Churches today should make sure that every driver is listed on the church's insurance or that they have been documented somewhere as an authorized driver to transport church members, visitors and friends to and from various church related events and functions. In addition to securing ample insurance upon drivers, each van should also carry a specified amount of insurance as required by their particular state. Please also take into consideration the actual insurance payment verses the insurance deductible. Know that the lower your insurance deductible is, the higher the insurance payment is going to be. All insurance information should be kept at fingertip with a copy in the vehicles, a copy in the church file and the original documents in a safe or offsite safety deposit box.

The third area to be address is the van maintenance, maintaining the van's ability to perform. Okay, we have a driver and we have insurance, but who maintains the vehicles? It is not as easy or as simple as some suggest putting in gasoline, antifreeze, and oil. Regular maintenance and preventative maintenance should be performed on all vehicles. Normal records and logging

Commentary for the new Pastor

the performed service should be kept in addition to the next scheduled appointment. It should be done for these areas but not limited to: complete coolant flushing, regular oil, filter and lube change, necessary aliments, tire rotations, normal washings and interior cleanings, headlamps and tail lamp inspection as well as other annual check-ups by qualified personnel. It is an embarrassment for the church van or bus to be immobile on the side of the highway due to lack of maintenance.

The fourth point of consideration is the said location that the van is sent to and what is the geographical location that most members require transportation? As a matter of fact, what is the specific area that the church has considered to evangelize that the van ministry is now to participate in? Each ministry needs to analyze what area the van ministry is most needed in, in order to be more accurate, economical, and precise in ministry. It is advantageous to consider this so that those who desire to worship can and will be able to without the worries of transportation.

The final statement in regards to the church transportation is the communication with the van in order to schedule parishioners for transportation and being able to communicate with the van after it has been dispatched. Question, is there some form of communication device located in the van? Is there a walkie-talkie, CB radio, and a Cellular telephone or paging device? In order to accurately perform and meet various standards that the ministry has employed for transportation, communication is going to be vastly important. Why? So that the van driver doesn't have to make unnecessary stops or return to the same location more than once on any given day, and if there happens to be an emergency that warrants communication with or from the driver, home base, or any other emergency service.

Van Ministry

Concluding request

Now, as a closing thought, please take into consideration the commitment that is needed from all qualified drivers in order to make the van ministry a successful piece and entity to the churches ministry. The van ministry in my opinion, is to ensure safe, accurate, dependable transportation for all who are in need of this service, for the not so typical or traditional Church Worship.

CHAPTER NINETEEN

Compensation for Employees

For the labourer is worthy of his hire. (Luke 10:7b)

EVERYBODY WANTS TO GET PAID

Well, it can honestly be stated, everyone wants to receive their paycheck on time, even church employees. The Church employees desire to be compensated, as in making some money and let me remind you of this detail: church folk or not. Church employees want their money at the end of the pay period (*as any other corporate employee*) if not making a request to receive it before the pay period is complete. Advancing the church employees compensation should not be a general practice within the ministry.

Thou shalt not muzzle the ox that treadeth out the corn. And, The labourer is worthy of his reward. (1 Timothy 5:18)

Commentary for the new Pastor

Financial compensation for church employees is always a strenuous assignment, because every church employee salary is determined basically by the tithe and general offering of the Church and then their qualifications are taken into consideration. If the church's tithe and general offering is consistently low, then there is a good chance that the employee's salary may also be low. If offerings are lower than the church's budget has determined, then there may need to be some hard financial adjustments made with the salaries of the employees or possibly even their positions may need to be eliminated, downsized and/or reevaluated in order to help meet the budget. The church is not a retail department store or food and restaurant chain that has the ability to drive the cost and sales of a product. The church is at the mercy of their members to spiritually recognize the vision of the church and to contribute cheerfully and regularly.

Monetary payments for church employees can be an assignment that is difficult to fulfill, the main reason being, there are no pre-set standards of salaries to follow, other than that particular church's *ability or desire* to compensate. The Church is not like corporate America, which suggests: *lets compare positions to the National Labor Industry.* Understand that, there is not a nationwide chart that equally compares your ministry to other ministries, because each ministry knows what they are capable of performing according to their own budget. The general point of consideration here again is, people talk and always compare what they are receiving as compensation to what someone else is getting elsewhere *(even within the ministry)* but remember each ministry is different. Regardless to what a church is able to do or not do they should never engage themselves into a price

Compensation for Employees

war with other ministries or a tug-o-war with which employee should receive a higher salary.

> Matthew 20:1–20, (excerpts only) For the kingdom of heaven is like unto a man that is an householder, which went out early in the morning to hire labourers into his vineyard. And when he had agreed with the labourers for a penny a day, he sent them into his vineyard. And he went out about the third hour, Again, about the sixth and ninth hour, and about the eleventh hour he went out. Verse 9–10 And when they came, that were hired about the eleventh hour, they received every man a penny. But when the first came, they supposed that they should have received more; and they likewise received every man a penny.

A Church which possesses more than two employees, in my opinion open the flood gates to three main themes that must be considered, however, understand that it is not limited to these three in its' entirety. Each church or ministry must make appropriations according to their own budget and employee manuals.

First, the Pastor and administration should decide if the church employees are going to be hourly or salaried with the church's best interest taken into consideration first. There are some positions that warrant both, yet the Pastor, Comptroller, and/or Human Resource Director will set in order job descriptions and standards prior to a person being hired, which includes determining if their position is going to be hourly or salary. Whether a person is hourly or salary should be established by the needs of the church and not with regards to a person's availability, taking into consideration any necessary pros and cons to that person and that particular position.

Commentary for the new Pastor

Definition of Hourly and Salary

If a person is hourly *(paid one flat rate per hour worked, multiplied by the hours worked for the week and then disbursed in the form of a paycheck either weekly or bi-weekly)*, they may clock in and then clock out manually. They are tracked for time by the time card as it is marked or punched. It is good to have hourly employees for they are paid for their actual time working on the church site. If they didn't clock in and out, they are not compensated for their labor performed. As a matter of fact, for hourly employees, if ever there were a need to cut time back or *(if allowed)* make time up, it can be seen and appropriately adjusted through this method.

However, if a person is salary *(one flat rate per year, divided in to each month and disbursed either weekly or biweekly)*, they are getting paid regardless to the number of hours that he or she works. If they work 30 hours per week they receive said dollars and if they work 70 hours a week they receive the same said dollars. If a person works salary they are not required to clock in and out (maybe writing their time in) for they may find themselves working more than a regular 40–hour workweek.

The second article that needs to be considered is the rules and regulations that pertain unto the Internal Revenue Service state, local, and city taxes. Many churches's are not aware and/or are not abiding by the said regulations for deducting the necessary taxes for each employee. Actually if the church is failing to take out taxes, (which they are not obligated to do), then a 1099 form should be issued at the end of each calendar year so that the employee can file proper taxes. Every employee has the right to declare, for their tax purpose 0 or 4 for the dollar amount to be withheld. Here is an additional bonus, be careful

Compensation for Employees

of employing senior workers who may be receiving their Social Security benefits, their salary from the church may affect their amount received each month.

Since so many rules, (according to each state), vary and change regularly, it is good for every church to consider employing a Certified Public Accountant to do the church payroll (if there is no one on staff qualified), which includes filing each individual taxes and issuing the necessary document at the end of the same year. Actually, they may even become responsible for mailing the checks weekly to each employee of the church.

The third piece of information that should be considered is the annual raises, seasonal bonuses, and paid time off. Yes, they all go together in some form and the church employees do anticipate them as other corporations. Most secular companies have a 90-day probationary period that each employee must pass then after that period a general increase is typically given averaging from 3–10 percent for the year. They can apply to the Ministry personnel for an additional increase that is if the head of the human resource department or pastor deems it befitting. However, there is a thriving force within Church employees, the moment the offering increases they outspokenly anticipate a increase in pay, whether their probationary period is fulfilled or if it is during their review time or not. The more employees you have the more it will be necessary to operate a certain portion of ministry as a business; which includes the hiring and dismissal of employees as well monetary salaries, even addressing tax deductions, time cards and sheets to receiving bonuses and pay cuts. Know that there are other means for compensation for the church employee, which are, but not limited to, gift certificates, yearly bonuses, time off with pay, food vouchers and various incentives.

CHAPTER TWENTY

Expectation of the Pastor

A bishop then must be blameless, the husband of one wife, vigilant, sober, of good behavior, given to hospitality, apt to teach; Not given to wine, no striker, not greedy of filthy lucre; but patient, not a brawler not covetous; One that ruleth well his own house, having his children in subjection with all gravity. (1 Timothy 3:2–4)

DID GOD SEND YOU, OR DID THE MEMBERS CALL YOU?

Now that you are the pastor, well, actually the pastor—elect, as some would describe you and for which I am also sure that someone has reminded you of, I need to ask a question. Has it been discussed with you during an interview, officers meeting, or church meeting what the current church members and officers have projected or even agreed upon, to what your ministerial responsibilities are as well as their expectations for you?

Commentary for the new Pastor

An early special note: As you and God have communed together to determine where the ministry should go and what your responsibilities should be; so have the church officers, pulpit committee and church members convened together regarding what they would like and even expect from their pastor—elect. Who will you listen to?

Typically, expectations or requirements have been preestablished by the "pulpit committee and/or church officers". There has been sacred time devoted to, studied and even followed to the T or I when looking to secure a pastor for *"their"* particular church. Bluntly speaking, because of this, you should know what is expected of you prior to your commitment to the church regardless of what you see and what has been promised to you. Every pastor should be knowledgeable of such documents to avoid encountering major migraine headaches because of particular individuals or unique situations.

As a matter of fact, allow me to take some time to list a few eye openers that each pastor or pastor—elect should concern himself or herself with as he or she accepts his or her new assignment.

1. everyone did not vote against you and neither did everyone vote for you
2. those who served the church on the pulpit committee may not surrender their authority willingly
3. you and the leadership will determine how long the marriage remains blissful and vibrant
4. don't be surprised if members who have left don't reinstate

Expectation of the Pastor

5. it takes time to build a ministry, it is your administrative skills that will ease the burden of this task
6. you are going to need to rely completely on the Holy Spirit more so than charisma, excitement, and intellect.

Question, what are your responsibilities and who has attempted to assign them to you? What are your expectations for yourself and what are the expectations that the church leadership has placed upon you? I hope that you grasp the fact that there is a difference between pastoral expectations and responsibilities. Expectations from my perspective are what people from outside your circle have suggested and hoped for you to achieve and accomplish, *which makes them the hero* and then responsibilities or everyday tasks are that you are required to perform for the general upkeep and overall spiritual maintenance of the ministry *which keeps you at a certain spiritual level with God.*

Little things to know and ask

Every minister and especially pastor should know what their responsibilities are as it relates to the church administration and providing the necessary spiritual leadership. Pastor, know if you are responsible or expected to serve communion to the members of the congregation or if the associate ministers and deacons are responsible. Distinguish if you are responsible or expected to go and visit every sick person in the hospital, nursing home, prison, or rehabilitation center or if the deacons and hospital committee personnel will be notified first? Be knowledgeable about your responsibilities verses their expectations in the beginning; for there could very well be an evaluating committee after each year that someone has forgotten to tell you about.

Commentary for the new Pastor

Pastors and Contracts

In discovering your responsibilities, also know if you are under any contract and if so, know the term that is legally binding. There are many churches in United States of America that continue to imprison and control their pastor under contract. Many times these contracts are one sided, meaning in one person or groups best interest and not mutually for each party represented. Contracts vary in provisions; unfortunately some pastors are under contract from year to year, very few are from three years or more, which limits the commitment of benefits.

A contract suggests, that if the church members or officers are not pleased with the growth and performance of the church and or the minister under the elected administration, then they may recommend dismissing the pastor without incident at the end of the contract or within the contract period. *Yes, boldly put, given the holy-boot.* If you are under contract, know the pros and cons as it relates to you, your future, and the scenery of your family in case of you being relocated to or from another city and state. It is also very advantageous to review the details of the contract in comparison with the church by-laws. The church bylaws vs. the pastoral contract may lock horns in respect to which has jurisdiction over your tenure.

... but what about the compensation

Every pastor should also want to know his or her salary and total benefit package especially if this is listed within the contract. It is vitally important to know what is included and what is excluded. What is current and what is projected? The biblical principal for each pastor's compensation is for the ministry to be as generous as possible, especially since Paul said for those that preach the gospel should live of the gospel.

Expectation of the Pastor

1 Corinthians 9:11–14, If we have sown unto you spiritual things, is it a great thing if we shall reap your carnal things? If others be partakers of this power over you, are not we rather? Nevertheless we have not used this power; but suffer all things, lest we should hinder the gospel of Christ. Do ye not know that they which minister about holy things live of the things of the temple? And they which wait at the altar are partakers of the altar? Even so hath the Lord ordained that they which preach the gospel should live of the gospel.

Some churches are able to support more than a generous salary, in addition to the health benefits. Others have implemented a housing allowance, an automobile stipend, or book allowance, to name a few. If you convene at the table to discuss these options, know what is required for you to provide a respectable standard of living for yourself and family (don't be scared or intimidated to make your request known, and neither become arrogant and so demanding that your professionalism is called into question).

Not everyone is concerned with or for the welfare of the pastor even though it is a biblical responsibility. Some congregants and officers think that he should still live in poverty or work in the secular arena like them; this is not true; so don't let the devil fool you or them. God's word describes that we should not muzzle the ox that treads out the corn.

Yet, the officers and church members expectation should quickly be addressed and brought into perspective with the pastor and church leaders vision. Yes, with God all things are possible, but the people should come to terms with themselves that:

a) the pastor is not God, only his mouthpiece/prophet/servant

Commentary for the new Pastor

b) that the pastor is going to come in within a weeks time and straighten up all the mess they created when there was no pastor, and my favorite

c) the officers and church members can not hold and/ or expect the current pastor to do what the other pastor failed to do. Too often a church's expectation is unrealistic to the purpose and vision of God in that particular pastor's life.

Notice a partial list of expectations, verses real responsibilities.

TYPICAL MEMBER AND CHURCH EXPECTATIONS

- To visit every sick and shut in member weekly and to know their addresses by heart
- To neglect your family, never have family time, but always be accessible for the church family
- To recite every church members name, address, phone number, join date and family member name
- To go to every hospital, nursing home, jail, board of education, rehabilitation center
- To live on honey, locusts, and spring water
- To perform marriages of members and non-members, bury the dead, and counsel the entire city
- To preach like Paul, sing like Silas, Pray like Peter, live like Jesus
- Never get upset or raise your voice
- To decline every raise and opportunity for advancement

Expectation of the Pastor

GENERAL BIBLICAL RESPONSIBILITIES:

- feed the flock of God
- equip the saints for the work of the ministry
- set in order the things that they are wanting
- to be partakers of the first fruits
- follow Christ, the originator of fellowship

What I am implying in this chapter is, people's expectations verses God's responsibilities are totally different and it needs to be addressed from a ministerial position, instead of being caught up in the hype of being the P-A-S-TO-R. *Don't allow your zeal for Pastoring to cause you and your family spiritual and economical woes.* Pastoring will cause a person's adrenaline to pump hard and fast, moving about in the flesh and possibly miss what God is saying in the spirit.

Now know this, not only can a Pastor be overwhelmed with the congregation's expectations, but he or she will assuredly have to face his or her own expectations also. For each Pastor will set goals for his or her ministry and then pray that God's hand of guidance rests upon him or her in accomplishing their goals. Every *"real"* Pastor has to set up goals for the ministry and the unfortunate thing is, people fail to know or consider the type of pressure that other people require upon him or her besides their own expectations.

> *Note: No Pastor plans to fail in reaching, ministering, teaching or fulfilling the desires he or she has for himself and those that the*

Commentary for the new Pastor

congregation has discussed and considered, but remind yourself that everyone does not want you to succeed.

Every pastor should know and practice his or her requirements and responsibilities without having to be told. Pastoring should not be taken as an opportunity to parade through an amusement park. With ministry, it should be facts before fantasy, evidence before excitement, determination before delight, godliness before gratification. Why, because we will die and will have been buried twice before we are able to fulfill every expectation of our beloved church members. Therefore, the only expectations that should be of a primary concern of yours as a pastor, is what God expects of you as a Christian and a leader.

God's expectations of His Pastor:

Titus 1:6–9, An elder must be blameless, the husband of but one wife, a man whose children believe and are not open to the charge of being wild and disobedient. Since an overseer is entrusted with God's work, he must be blameless-not overbearing, not quick-tempered, not given to drunkenness, not violent, not pursuing dishonest gain. Rather he must be hospitable, one who loves what is good, who is self-controlled, upright, holy and disciplined. He must hold firmly to the trustworthy message as it has been taught, so that he can encourage others by sound doctrine and refute those who oppose it. (NIV)

(Summation) A pastor must live the life that they are embarking upon preaching, teaching and exhorting others to do. Their character must be as admirable as the wonders of the world.

2 Timothy 4:2, Preach the word; be instant in season, out of season; reprove, rebuke, exhort with all longsuffering and doctrine.

Expectation of the Pastor

(Summation) Regardless to what the conditions or elements of spiritual society presents to you while you are in ministry, as the pastor you still must be able to give a life changing message applicable to where men and women are. This must be achieved, while pushing your emotions and desires aside.

Philippians 3:17, Brethren, be followers together of me, and mark them which walk so as ye have us for an ensample.

(Summation) Every Pastor is a pattern. The same way that a tailor or seamstress would use a paper pattern to cut and then sew a piece of fabric to make a garment, Pastors should be prepared to be an example for others to follow in order to be Christ-like. Question, what type of a pattern are you?

2 Timothy 2:6, The husbandman that laboureth must be first partaker of the fruits.

(Summation) There are some Christians who believe that the pastor should constantly live in poverty and scrap and scratch his way into a blessing, when in fact God says to be the first partaker of where you've labored. Learn how to receive a blessing, as you have been a blessing.

Titus 2:1, But speak thou the things which become sound doctrine.

(Summation) Because there are so many false prophets in the world and a great falling away from the truth, every pastor must ensure themselves as well as others that they are first qualified and secondly prepared to give instruction and correction but most of all a firm and solid theology of Christ.

Reassure yourself if you must but know the vast difference between God placing various expectations within your spirit and the church members implying expectations upon your ministry.

Commentary for the new Pastor

Ask yourself, is it a burden to do or a burden weighing down; is it a task to accomplish or a task to do? Whatever responsibility God has prearranged for you to do, remember that he has also given you the ability to achieve and weather the storms of ministry with minimum damage.

Questions that are generally asked by the Pulpit Committee, Search Committee, Church Council or Deacon ministry

1. Why do you want to become the pastor of XYZ church?
2. When did you receive Christ as your personal Lord and Savior?
3. How long have you been in the ministry and when were you licensed?
4. Are you an Ordained minister and what was the type of council that catechized you?
5. Are you married, and is your spouse a believer in Christ?
6. How active are you or were you as an associate minister?
7. Do you have your pastors' blessings upon you and your ministry?
8. What specific bible based programs addressing the youth, Christian education, evangelism, outreach ministry, senior members, childcare, etc.
9. Are you a fundamentalist or a liberalist?

Commentary for the new Pastor

10. Have you and where did you receive any formal ministerial training, including college?
11. Which version of the bible are you accustom to teaching and preaching from and why?
12. Are you opposed to sharing or fellowshipping in church conventions?
13. How do you proposed to deal with conflict in the church, especially amongst church leadership?
14. Do you believe in and support the five-fold ministry and do you believe they are active today?
15. What are your thoughts on tongue speaking, is it essential for salvation?
16. Is there a need anointing oil and when, if so?
17. What is the position and authority of the Deacons, Elders, Stewards, Trustee and other leaders?
18. What is the role of women in the church?
19. Is there a place for women pastors and preachers, and what is your personal and biblical view?
20. How do you propose to deal with sin in the church amongst its members?
21. List your church music preference.
22. Are you willing to relocate?
23. What are your salary expectation and housing requirements?
24. Are you willing to continue your ministerial training and education?
25. Do you have any current health problems?
26. Is your personal credit history satisfactory?

Questions that are generally asked by the Pulpit Committee, Search Committee, Church Council or Deacon ministry

27. What are your doctrinal views on Salvation, the Holy Spirit, the Trinity, Sanctification, etc?
28. What is your view on tithing, offerings and gifts unto the church?
29. How important is church, local and foreign missions?

Please consider this only as a partial list of possible question that could be asked by any search committee, pulpit committee or deacon ministry. The inquiry of questions could take place at the interview, during the candidating period or once the helm of the ministry is under the ministers' pastorate. The most important issue or series of questions for each minister who begins a new pastorate to be concerned with is, being able to confidently respond to any query that God makes regarding their call to ministry, their ability and willingness to follow while leading the people of God, all while being intimately in touch with his or her inner being and conscience.

Read What Other Pastors Are Recommending

What a planting Pastor needs to know

The call of God to a pastor is the highest call a man or woman can ever receive. Pastors who are called to lead a people and manifest the vision that God has placed in their hearts are initially confronted with several oppositions even before taking on the responsibility of the assignment. These oppositions do exist in all areas, states, cities, towns, and our country. They are derived from Ephesians 6:12, "For we wrestle not against flesh and blood, but against principalities, against powers, against the rulers of the darkness of this world, against spiritual wickedness in high places." The pastor must spy the area. The way he will do this is through the demographics of the area issued by the last census. Then he must obtain a need assessment from the local social security department. In order for that pastor to effectively fulfill the call of God, he must know what demonic forces he

Commentary for the new Pastor

will be fighting against. Once he has completed the demographic study and compiled the needs assessment, he then must use what I call the Nehemiah format for rebuilding and developing a community God's way. I believe God, will continue to anoint and elevate your Ministry. God Bless!

Pastor Darren L. Gay Sr.
Higher Way Full Gospel Baptist Church
Waverly VA.

Words to the new Pastor from a seasoned Pastor

Rev. Marc Neal has asked me to write the following as words of inspiration to young pastors and new pastors.

Learn to cultivate a relationship with the Holy Spirit. He wants to fellowship with you and will speak to your spirit about how to effectively lead God's people. Check out the following passages: John 14:16–17, 26; 15:26; 16:13– 15; Acts 13:2; 15:28; 16:6–10; Romans 8:14–17; 1 Corinthians 2:9–12; and finally, 2 Corinthians 13:14. The Holy Spirit still speaks through the Scriptures, through situations, at times through people, but most definitely to our spirit in line with the Scriptures and the will of God. He will not violate what God has said. When we get to know His voice, vision is imparted, timing becomes essential, and implementation of the will of God a must.

There are written and unwritten rules in churches that do not come to the front when you first accept a church. Find out what those rules are before you sign any document that you may later regret signing. The late Dr. Sandy F. Ray, in an suggested that when we preach the Word of the Lord, a piece of paper—referring to

Read What Other Pastors Are Recommending

a contract with pastoral benefits—will be taken care of by the Lord. That is to say that God will see to it that the people you pastor do not mistreat you. You love them and they will love you back—in most cases.

If the Holy Spirit has pointed this congregation out to you as the place to work, go in knowing that He has placed you there for a purpose: to lead and feed His people. The words of Jesus to Peter—who represents all pastors over the centuries—in 1 John 21:15–18 say that our responsibility as pastors is to lead and feed the flock. There will be people who resist the food, perhaps they are goats and not lambs and sheep; sheep can be led (taught). The apostle Paul and Peter remind us of the awesome task of being entrusted with the souls placed in our care. The writer of Hebrews is no less vocal when his advice to the congregation is to follow the pastor (those who have the responsibility of following where you lead) so that they do not make your job hard (Acts 20:28; 1 Peter 5:1–7; Hebrews 13:7, 17).

One good stroll through 1 Thessalonians 5 will tell you that verses 12–14 call for a mutual support system that can easily exist between the senior pastor and the parishioners. The pastor leads, is held in high esteem, and is obeyed— the congregation keeping an atmosphere of peace alive; the congregation follows and helps keep the unruly in line. What a blessing it is to have the Holy Spirit leading you as you lead God's people. You get to teach and model caring skills, pass it on to those who are to help you with congregational care: associate staff preachers, deacon ministry, trustee ministry, and other spiritually gifted volunteer leaders who aid you with this great responsibility. It is nothing to avoid, because there is so much to be enjoyed: watching people grow in their spiritual maturity.

Commentary for the new Pastor

Don't ever start a fight. You will never be able to win it. The Lord has His own way of revealing hidden agendas and folks who "throw rocks and hide their hands." Wait until He puts the information you need in your hands, wait for His timing, and then unveil God's plans for correction and instruction in righteousness. *Cast your cares upon Him* is the message pastors must keep in mind. The Lord has a way of placing the right people in your path; people who love Him so much that they will properly love their pastor, warn the pastor of impending danger from the gallery—most of the time as confirmation that the Holy Spirit has already warned you.

Remember that God would not have picked this congregation out for you if He did not believe you could handle the work with His help. Ask the Lord for the wisdom you need to lead and once He grants it to you (and He is no shorter than His word—see James 1:5), and then use it to enhance the Kingdom of God and Christ. I believe that Paul sums it up for us whether with it is a new work or you are a seasoned veteran *"I can do all things through Christ which strengtheneth me."* (Philippians 4:13).

God bless you in your work.
T. DeWitt Smith, Jr., D. Min., Senior Pastor
West Hunter Street Baptist Church
Atlanta, GA

About the Author

Bishop Marc L. Neal is a native of Akron, Ohio and is currently serving as the senior pastor of Dominion Family Church and the Presiding Prelate of Come Alive Ministry International Fellowship spanning over sixteen countries. He

Read What Other Pastors Are Recommending

is a sought after lecture, facilitator and trainer. He is the author of: Keys to Identifying Your Call and The Heart of a Champion. He is a member of the advisory team for the Sandberg Leadership Center of Ashland Theological Seminary. He has received many awards for outstanding leadership, ecumenical and humanitarian service. His Christian educational background includes studies with, Moody Bible Institute, Ashland Theological Seminary, Saint Thomas Christian College and Infinity Bible Seminary.

Final thoughts:

Each pastor will have his or her own set of challenges to mull over as they move into the operative position that God has ordered them. No pastor is exempt from confrontation for the enemy is non-biased. Yet, it is not the challenges that should be our concern, as it is the personal and spiritual preparation of the pastor and how he or she will focus upon the solution for the concerns presented before him or her. Surely, each pastor must be prepared. Being prepared includes listening, giving a soft answering, quality concencrative time with God, building experience, surrounding one's self with the appropriate inner-circle, and obtaining the proper level of higher learning.

Now that you are in what may be your first and/or only appointment for ministry (then again it may not be), it becomes obviously imperative for you to ensure that you are well prepared personally for multiple experiences and situations that confront the administration of the church. If you are not spiritually, mentally, and emotionally spirited and healthy, then confronting some of the issues that await you in your ministry may overwhelm you or move pass you, as it has other pastors throughout the country. Pastoring a thriving ministry, desiring to grow personally

Commentary for the new Pastor

and keeping an equal balance of family time is a strenuous feat and becomes more wearisome when the leader fails in leading and administrating. Failing to contend for the faith by setting in order the things that are wanting will become as dangerous as a man parachuting out of an airplane at 20,000 feet high, without the parachute.

- Knowing, no weapon formed against you shall prosper is one thing, but being able to survive the wounds of the battle is another.
- Realizing that God will keep those in perfect peace whose mind is stay upon him, is a worthy saying, but progressing through and beyond the distractions of ministry is another.
- Accepting the verses of scripture that remind us that God will never leave thee nor forsake thee, or the verse that reminds us that there is a friend that sticks closer than any brother is very encouraging. However, feeling Gods presence in the midst of opposition and confusion when the spirit of loneliness hovers over us is another issue.

Now that you are there, what's next for you and the ministry where you are? I know you are excited and the adrenaline is soaring through your anatomy, but what's next? Question, are you first sure that God sent you there, provided this opportunity for you, predestinated you to be where you are or was it simply your resume' that appeared profitable for the ministry that sought you or you sought out? Assuredly, you must know, as you know your name that Jehovah God has set you in the midst of those wailing men and women, and you know without reservation

Read What Other Pastors Are Recommending

your specific purpose. Once you know your destiny, you can fulfill your purpose with the joy and confidence that God will manifest himself in your ministry to honor his name perpetually. Take the opportunity to first reevaluate your call and then finally confer that you are where God desires you to be. And finally move harmlessly but yet wisely through the gates of the congregation to know them and the ministry where you are serving.

God's riches blessings rest upon you as you continue your plight for the salvation of the lost and the edification of the saints, but most of all the glorification of God our Father, through Jesus Christ our Lord.

Your friend,
Bishop Marc L. Neal

To book Bishop Marc L. Neal for speaking engagments please email: dunamis137@aol.com

www.ingramcontent.com/pod-product-compliance
Lightning Source LLC
Chambersburg PA
CBHW060517100426
42743CB00009B/1352